# WOMEN IN THE LIFE OF JESUS

D0450481

# WOMEN IN THE LIFE OF JESUS

## VICTOR BOOKS®

A DIVISION OF SCRIPTURE PRESS PUBLICATIONS INC.
USA CANADA ENGLAND

*Third printing, 1988*

Scripture verses quoted are taken from *The New King James Version* (NKJV),
© 1979, 1980, 1982, Thomas Nelson, Inc., Publishers; the *Holy Bible, New International Version* (NIV), © 1973, 1978, 1984, International Bible Society, used by permission of Zondervan Bible Publishers; and the *King James Version* (KJV).


Recommended Dewey Decimal Classification: 225.922
Suggested Subject Heading: BIBLE, N.T.—BIOGRAPHY

Library of Congress Catalog Card Number: 86-60855
ISBN: 0-89693-254-0

© 1986 by SP Publications, Inc. All rights reserved. Printed in the United States of America.
No part of this book may be reproduced without written permission, except for brief quotations in books, critical articles, and reviews.

VICTOR BOOKS
A division of SP Publications, Inc.
        Wheaton, Illinois 60187

# •CONTENTS•

*Recognition to Karen Seemuth*
*for assistance*
*in researching and formulating*
*parts of this book.*

# •BEFORE YOU BEGIN•

People who gather together for Bible study are likely to be at different places in their spiritual lives, and their study materials should be flexible enough to meet their different needs. This book is designed to be used as a Bible study guide for such groups in homes or churches. It can also be used by individuals who are studying on their own. The lessons are written in five distinct sections, so that they can be used in a variety of situations. Groups and individuals alike can choose to use the elements they find most useful in the order they find most beneficial.

These studies will help you learn some new truths from the Bible as well as how to dig out those truths. You will learn not only *what* the Bible says, but how to use Scripture to deepen your relationship with Jesus Christ by obeying it and applying it in daily living. These studies will also provide an opportunity for potential leaders to learn how to lead a discussion in a nonthreatening setting.

**What You'll Need**
For each study you will need a Bible and this Bible study guide. You might also want to have a notebook in which to record your thoughts and discoveries from your personal study and group meetings. A notebook could also be used to record prayer requests from the group.

**The Sections**

*Food for Thought.* This is a devotional narrative that introduces the topic, person, or passage featured in the lesson. There are several ways it can be used. Each person could read it before coming to the group meeting, and someone could briefly summarize it at the beginning. It could be read silently by each person at the beginning of the session, or it could be read aloud, by one or several group members. (Suggested time: 10 minutes)

*Talking It Over.* This section contains discussion questions to help you review what you learn in Food for Thought. There are also questions to help you apply the narrative's truths to daily life. The person who leads the discussion of these questions need not be a trained or experienced teacher. All that is needed is someone to keep things moving and facilitate group interaction. (Suggested time: 30 minutes)

*Praying It Through.* This is a list of suggestions for prayer based on the lesson. You may want to use all the suggestions or eliminate some in order to leave more time for personal sharing and prayer requests. (Suggested time: 20 minutes)

*Digging Deeper.* The questions in this section are also related to the passage, topic, or character from the lesson. But they will not always be limited to the exact passage or character from Food for Thought. Passages and characters from both the Old and New Testaments will appear in this section, in order to show how God has worked through *all* of history in people's lives. These questions will require a little more thinking and some digging into Scripture, as well as some use of Bible study tools. Participants will be stretched as they become experienced in the "how-tos" of Bible study. (Suggested time: 45 minutes)

*Tool Chest.* The Tool Chest contains a description of a specific type of Bible study help and includes an explanation of how it is used. An example of the tool is given, and an example of it or excerpt from it is usually included in the Digging Deeper study.

The Bible study helps in the Tool Chest can be purchased by anyone who desires to build a basic library of Bible study reference books and other tools. They would also be good additions to a church library. Some are reasonably inexpensive, but others are quite expensive. A few may be available in your local library or in a seminary or college library. A group might decide to purchase one tool during each series and build a corporate tool chest for all the members of the group to use. You can never be too young a Christian to begin to master Bible study helps, nor can you be too old to learn new methods of rightly dividing the Word of truth.

The Tool Chest won't be used during the group time unless the leader wishes to draw special attention to it. Those who will be using the Digging Deeper study should read the Tool Chest on their own before or after doing the study.

**Options for Group Use**
Different groups, made up of people at diverse stages of spiritual growth, will want to use the elements in this book in different ways. Here are a few suggestions to get you started, but be creative and sensitive to your group's needs.

□ Spend 5-15 minutes at the beginning of the group time introducing yourselves and having group members answer an icebreaker question. (Sample icebreaker questions are included under Tips for Leaders.)

□ Extend the prayer time to include sharing of prayer requests, praise items, or things group members have learned recently in their times of personal Bible study.

□ The leader could choose questions for discussion from the Digging Deeper section based on whether participants have prepared ahead of time or not.

□ The entire group could break into smaller groups to allow different groups to use different sections. (The smaller groups could move to other rooms in the home or church where you are meeting.)

The key thing to remember is that you *don't have to feel obliged to use everything*. Pick what you or your group needs. Omit questions or reword them if you wish. Feel free to be flexible!

**Tips for Leaders**
*Preparation.*
1. Pray for the Holy Spirit's help as you study, that you will be equipped to teach the lesson and make it appealing and applicable.

2. Read through the entire lesson and any Bible passages or verses that are mentioned. Answer all the questions.

3. Become familiar enough with the lesson that, if time in the group is running out, you know which questions could most easily be left out.

4. Gather all the items you will need for the study: name tags, extra pens, extra Bibles.

*The Meeting.*

1. Start and end on time.

2. Have everyone wear a name tag until group members know one another's names.

3. Have each person introduce himself or herself, or ask regular attenders to introduce guests.

4. For each meeting, pick an icebreaker question or other activity to help group members get to know one another better.

5. Use any good ideas to make the everyone feel comfortable.

*The Discussion.*

1. Ask the questions, but try to let the group answer. Don't be afraid of silence. Reword the question if it is unclear to the group or answer it yourself to clarify.

2. Encourage everyone to participate. If someone is shy, ask that person to answer an opinion question or other nonthreatening question. If someone tends to monopolize the discussion, thank that person for his or her contribution and ask if someone else has anything he or she would like to add. (Or ask that person to make the coffee!)

3. If someone gives an incorrect answer, don't bluntly or tactlessly tell him or her so. If it is partly right, reinforce that. Ask if anyone else has any thoughts on the subject. (Disagree agreeably!)

4. Avoid tangents. If someone is getting off the subject, ask that person how his or her point relates to the lesson.

5. Don't feel threatened if someone asks a question you can't answer. Tell the person you don't know but will find out before the next meeting—then be sure to find out! Or ask if someone would like to research and present the answer at the group's next meeting.

*Icebreaker Questions.*

The purpose of these icebreaker questions is to help the people in your group get to know one another over the course of the study. The questions you use when your group members don't know one another very well should be very general and nonthreatening. As time goes on, your questions can become more focused and specific. Always give group members the option of passing if they think a question is too personal.

What do you like to do for fun?
What is your favorite season? dessert? book?
What would be your ideal vacation?
What exciting thing happened to you this week?
What was the most memorable thing you did with your family when you were a child?
What one word best describes the way you feel today?
Tell three things you are thankful for.
Imagine that your house is on fire. What three things would you try to take with you on your way out?
If you were granted one wish, what would it be?
What experience of your past would you most enjoy reliving?
What quality do you most appreciate in a friend?
What is your pet peeve?
What is something you are learning to do or trying to get better at?
What is your greatest hope?
What is your greatest fear?
What one thing would you like to change about yourself?
What has been the greatest accomplishment of your life?
What has been the greatest disappointment of your life?

*Need More Help?*
Here is a list of books that contain helpful information on leading discussions and working in groups:

*How to Lead Small Group Bible Studies* (NavPress, 1982).
*Creative Bible Learning for Adults,* Monroe Marlowe and Bobbie Reed (Regal, 1977).
*Getting Together,* Em Griffin (InterVarsity Press, 1982).
*Good Things Come in Small Groups* (InterVarsity Press, 1985).

**One Last Thought**

This book is a tool you can use whether you have one or one hundred people who want to study the Bible and whether you have one or no teachers. Don't wait for a brilliant Bible study leader to appear—most such leaders acquired their skills by starting with a book like this and learning as they went along. Torrey said, "The best way to begin, is to begin." Happy beginnings!

# 1
## *Sinful Women*

## •FOOD FOR THOUGHT•

Women had a special place in the heart of the Lord Jesus. Think of it—they were the first at His birth, last at His cross, and first to be commanded to run and tell of His resurrection. Jesus gave dignity to women, who were treated little better than cattle by the nations around Israel. The Jews were not averse to keeping women at a pretty low level either. A good Jewish man would often begin his day by praying, "I thank Thee God I am not a Gentile, I am not a slave, I am not a woman!" Christ elevated women by securing a place for them in His own life and in the very heart of His ministry.

In this series of Bible studies, we will be looking at some of the sorrowing, sick, sexual, and successful women in Christ's life. We will study and think about the women in Jesus' stories and others who interacted with Him. We'll begin by thinking about a sinful woman.

Now if I were to ask you to pick someone to fit that description, whom would you choose? The woman at the well perhaps, or the poor creature dragged in front of Christ straight out of the bed of adultery? Many of us would say, "It has to be Mary of Magdala" (though the Bible leaves no record of her as a licentious woman, but rather as a demon-possessed woman who might well have been driven to such extremes). I'm sure it is a surprise to many of you to see I have chosen Mary of Nazareth! I hope this does not offend you.

I believe that Mary herself would be the first to acknowledge the fact that she qualifies to be the subject of this first study.

I firmly believe that Mary was the best woman that ever lived. But I also believe she was a sinner. Mary was a special lady. She was good—good enough to bear God's Son but not good enough to get to heaven without Him! Let's look at her life and try to hear the message she brings to us.

First of all she calls herself a "handmaiden of the Lord" (Luke 1:38). The word she uses is *doulē*, which means "slavegirl." "I am the Lord's slavegirl," she said of herself. Mary served the Lord. You can't serve someone you don't know, and you can't serve as a slave unless you have first been carried away captive. Mary's young, willing heart had undoubtedly been captured by her God. What does that mean? It means that Mary had believed the facts she had been taught about God. She believed He was majestic, mighty, and merciful (Luke 1:49-51). She had been well taught in the things of the Lord from her youth, a fact well evidenced by her own grasp of the Scriptures and also by the ministry of the Lord Jesus Christ Himself. "No man ever spoke like this Man" (John 7:46, NKJV), records John of Him who had received Mary's mother-help in His infancy. Scripture poured from His lips on a daily basis. I believe Mary had much to do with that! If we are to call ourselves handmaidens of the Lord, we must know the Lord we serve, and that involves a grasp of biblically revealed facts concerning His character and purpose.

Mary's soul, her whole being, magnified her Lord and not herself (Luke 1:46). What is more, her spirit rejoiced in God *her* "Saviour" (Luke 1:47).

Mary calls God her Saviour. Even though Gabriel assures her that God's favor rests upon her, Mary is called to be not the source of grace but the object of it.

We can all imagine what sort of woman she must have been to be called to become the earthly mother of the Christ, but Mary's deep humility and own sweet testimony confirm the fact of her human need. Only imperfect people need a Saviour. Only divinity is perfect.

That brings us to an obvious application. The very best people need a Saviour, because the very best people are sinners. It is as hard for some "good" people to believe that as it is for many to believe that Mary was a sinner. Yet there are good sinners! Does that sound like a contradiction? Good sinners sometimes find it difficult to see their need of God because they are almost good enough without Him! And yet a truly good person is ever conscious of his or her shortcomings. And that's exactly what the Bible teaches. We all "fall short of the glory of God" (Rom. 3:23, NIV). "There is none who does good" (and in case one of us thinks there is an exception, the Bible adds) "no, not one" (Ps. 14:3, NKJV). Good people concentrate not so much on asking God to forgive them for the things they have done that they shouldn't have done but rather on asking forgiveness for the things they haven't done that they ought to have done. A truly good person knows that all imperfection is sin.

But, you may ask, how do good people know these things? I'm glad you asked! They come to know them by reading His Word. "Be it unto me according to Thy Word" (Luke 1:38, KJV), Mary said to Gabriel. Mary, after all, was not only a handmaiden, she was a heartmaiden too. She was a woman of the Word.

Three times Mary is recorded as saying that she "treasured all these things in her heart." Her heart was a treasure chest, and her keen mind was the keeper of it. Mary was not only responsible to God, she was also reflective. She pondered the truths of the Lord until they made sense to her. She did not always understand them at first (Luke 1:43), but she remembered them.

It isn't easy to collect Jesus' sayings in your heart, because they are not always things you want to keep in mind. Mary "treasured *all* these things in her heart"—both the good words and the hard words. When Simeon told her that a sword would pierce her heart, she had no idea what he meant, but she remembered his words. When Jesus told her that the people who did His will were as mother and brothers to Him, she was surely hurt and confused, but she just as surely pondered it all in her heart. Being a handmaiden and a heartmaiden means you can end up being a hurtmaiden, but that's what Jesus loves about His very special people. They let *none* of His words fall to the ground, whatever the cost to themselves. The promises of God are easy to memorize, but the commands of Scripture are harder to treasure. Ask yourself: Am I the sort of woman who delights in pondering the warnings of the Word? If so, you can know Jesus will be delighted in you.

Being one of the Lord's special people, however, carries its own sacred consequences. The large sword of suffering in the shape of her Son's cross was to pierce Mary's very being. If you are superficial in your thinking, the very idea of being one of God's favored folk sounds like a grand idea. Jesus was God's very special Son, His favored child. "This is My beloved Son, in whom I am well pleased," God said (Matt. 3:17, NKJV). We need to be very careful before we say,

> "I want to be Your favorite child, Father!"
> "You do?" He may reply.
> "Yes, I really do; that sounds like fun!"
> "My favorite child like whom?"
> "Well, like Jesus."
> "Then flatten out your hands upon My cross, pile foot on foot that nails may pierce them through. Hang high, hang long above the blood-soaked turf and bear judgment deep upon your soul for others' sin. Then, go to hell, My child, My favorite child!
> "Now that doesn't sound like too much fun after all, does it?"

Mary had been promised by the angel that she would be the happiest of women, and yet she had to endure the cross of her Christ and discover the fellowship of His sufferings for herself. To say "behold the handmaid of the Lord, be it unto me according to Thy Word" is not the end of our problems. For many of us, as for Mary, it is sometimes only the beginning of them.

Yet Christ gives us His comfort. Even at the cross, He cared for His mother when His hands were tied—or to be more brutally accurate—nailed securely down. But think of it. Now His hands are gloriously free to reach our pierced hearts. Whether we must watch the death of our child as Mary did or stand idly by and watch one dear to us destroy himself or herself with drugs or bad choices, we know we have a God who revealed Himself in Christ as One who knows what suffering is and who will succor us in it (Heb. 4:15-16).

The last glimpse we have of Mary is very special. Taken into John's care and keeping, she doubtless heard the reports of her Son's resurrection. Her other children must have been converted sometime during this period, and Pentecost saw the family united, awaiting the coming of the Holy Spirit. When Joel's prophecy was fulfilled and the Holy Spirit was poured out upon God's men and "maidens," Mary was part of the infant church. No doubt she did her gracious part in nurturing Christ's bride even as she had nurtured the Bridegroom! We can picture her in our mind's eye in the fellowship of God's people praying to the Father through her Son, taking the bread and the wine reminding her of His death, and doing good for the poor and needy (Acts 2:42-45).

The record of Mary's life on earth ends as it began, with her soul magnifying the Lord, her spirit rejoicing in God her Saviour, and her body willingly given to be the earthly vehicle of His divine actions here on earth.

Mary has much to teach us. Few will ever be as good as she, and yet she called her Son her Saviour. Never again will any other woman know her unique call from God, and Jesus honored her for it. Yet in response to a woman exalting His mother above measure saying, "Blessed is the womb that bore You, and the breasts which nursed You!" He said, "More than that, blessed are those who hear the Word of God and keep it!" (Luke 11:27-28, NKJV)

The new relationships of the kingdom mean that you and I can enjoy His grace and favor too. We have the privilege of hearing His Word, and we must make the choice to treasure it in our hearts. Most importantly, we can respond to Him as Mary of Nazareth did and say, "Behold the handmaid of the Lord, be it unto me according to Your Word" (Luke 1:38, KJV).

# •TALKING IT OVER•

---

1. DISCUSS.                                           *15 minutes*

☐ (Handmaidens—Luke 1:38) What does Mary teach us about sin? servanthood? her Saviour?

☐ (Heartmaidens—Luke 1:38, 45) What does Mary teach us about the Word of God?

☐ (Hurtmaidens—Luke 2:24-35) What did you learn about God's favorite people today?

---

2. READ AND SHARE.                             *10 minutes*

In twos, choose either Acts 1:12-14 or Acts 2:16-18 and think about Mary being involved in the action. What thoughts do you have about that? Share with the group.

---

3. PRAY.                                              *5 minutes*

# • PRAYING IT THROUGH •

*Suggested
Times*

1. Individually, open your Bible to Mary's song (Luke 1:46-55) and read it to yourself. Find three things to praise God about—borrow Mary's words or use your own. As a group, praise God together.

*5 minutes*

2. Individually, choose one verse of Scripture from Mary's song—*ponder it*. In silent prayer, commit it to memory *now*. Share with the group your verse and why you chose it.

*6 minutes*

3. Pray short prayers for any you know who are watching loved ones suffer.

*6 minutes*

4. Meditate silently on this verse: "The Mighty One has done great things for me—holy is His name" (Luke 1:49, NIV).

*2 minutes*

5. Close by saying grace together—"The grace of the Lord Jesus, the love of God, and the fellowship of the Holy Spirit be with us all evermore. Amen."

*1 minute*

# •DIGGING DEEPER•

1. Look up all the following verses and compose one definition of sin.

   Job 33:27   Ephesians 2:1   1 John 3:4
   Romans 3:9, 23  James 4:17   1 John 5:17

2. There are several Greek words used to express the concept of sin. English also has a number of words that describe sin. Some of them are *disobedience, error, fault, guile, iniquity, transgression, trespass, ungodliness,* as well as *sin.* For this lesson we will look at just five of these English words: *SIN, TRESPASS, INIQUITY, GUILE,* and *TRANSGRESSION.*

   If we were to look up these five words in *An Expository Dictionary of New Testament Words* by W.E. Vine (Fleming Revell, 1940), we would find the original Greek word or words and their meanings. Look below at these Greek words and meanings and read through the Scripture reference that corresponds to each meaning. Write out each Scripture verse in your own words in the space provided.

**SIN**
 *hamartia*—a missing of the mark; James 4:17

 *hamartēma*—an act of disobedience; 2 Peter 1:9

**TRESPASS**
 *paraptōma*—a false step; Matthew 6:14-15

**INIQUITY**
*anomia*—lawlessness; Romans 6:19

*adikia*—unrighteousness; Acts 8:23

**GUILE**
*dolos*—deceit, a bait, snare; Acts 13:10

**TRANSGRESSION**
*parabasis*—a going aside, an overstepping; Romans 5:14

3. According to Romans 3:9-23 and 1 John 3:4, who is a sinner?

4. What effect does sin have on our lives? (Romans 6:23)

5. In Luke 1:38, Mary says, "I am the Lord's servant." The Greek word for servant is *doulē*, which can also be translated as hand-maiden, or bond-slave. Read Exodus 21:2-6. In Old Testament times, a person could sell himself as a slave for six years in order to pay off his debts. After the six years, he was granted his freedom. But if he had grown to love his master and wanted to remain, he could choose to remain the master's servant for life, and as a sign of this, his ear would be pierced. So there were two types of slaves—slaves out of obligation and slaves out of love. If you are a slave of Christ, are you a slave out of obligation or out of love?

6. How does a person become a slave of Christ?

7. What does it mean to be a slave of Christ?

8. Read Luke 1:46-55, the Magnificat. Why does Mary say she will be called blessed?

9. Why would you say *you* are blessed?

10. According to Acts 1:14, what sort of woman do you think Mary was?

11. How should we pray? What should be included in our prayers? (See 2 Chron. 7:14; Matt. 5:44; 6:5, 9; Luke 6:28; 1 Thes. 5:17; James 5:13, 16.)

12. Write a prayer, thanking God for the blessings you listed in question 9.

# •TOOL CHEST•
*(A Suggested Optional Resource)*

*WORD STUDY HELPS*
*An Expository Dictionary of New Testament Words* by W.E. Vine (Fleming Revell, 1940) is a very useful tool for those who have not studied New Testament Greek.

As you study in the New Testament you may come across words that you would like to study in more depth or words that you don't understand. All one needs to do is look up the English word in Vine's (as the book is commonly called). Just as in a regular dictionary, the words are listed in alphabetical order. Under the English word are listed the original Greek words for the English word, the meanings, and a number of Scripture references in which those Greek words appear. If there are other English words with similar meanings, Vine's will refer you to those also.

As with all Bible study tools, Vine's should be consulted only after you have thoroughly studied a passage on your own.

# 2
## *Sorrowing Women*

## •FOOD FOR THOUGHT•

"Why does God allow sorrow to visit my life, my home, and the lives of my loved ones?" inquired a tearful mother. "Isn't He big enough or brave enough to act on our behalf? And where did sorrow come from in the first place?" How many times have we heard that question asked? The Bible gives us an answer to the problem of suffering. The Scriptures tell us it all began in heaven. God created a beautiful angel—a minister of light called Lucifer, son of the dawn (Isa. 14:12-20). He decided he would not take orders from on high anymore, and at that moment disorder entered that angel's heart and sin was born. Sin is not being wholly subject to God, and Lucifer, son of the dawn, was cast out of heaven, and he secured the downfall of Adam and through him the human race. Sin has spoiled God's earth, and all who have lived have experienced the sorrow of it. The source of sorrow, then, is Satan himself.

But Christians cannot think about the source of sorrow without realizing that the Son of sorrow, Jesus Christ, is God's answer to the problem. Isaiah told us that God's Son would be "a man of sorrows and acquainted with grief" (Isa. 53:3, NKJV). Christianity answers the problem of suffering by revealing a God who appeared in Christ and who by suffering brought a race of rebellious creatures, including you and me, within reach of salvation (Isa. 53:10-12). Christians need only to look at the Cross to know we have a God who cares about those who sorrow and suffer.

Both the Old Testament and the New Testament tell of a God who has great compassion for the suffering. We see in the life and ministry of Jesus Christ a demonstration of that fact. For thirty-three years Jesus Christ walked on our earth, lived our life, felt our pain, and eventually died our death, but not before He had met sorrow and addressed it face to face. He overcame death itself at the cross and gave an answer to those who "were all their lifetime subject to bondage" (Heb. 2:15, NKJV). Christ is seen reaching out, particularly to sorrowing women. He actually cares for the lonely and rejected. Let's look at two particular aspects of suffering and see how Jesus reacted to them.

Let's start with loneliness. There are many women suffering today because they are lonely. Single women talk of an intimate loneliness that hurts. Married women have confessed a loneliness even while surrounded by friends or family. Some have even felt an isolation within their very marriage relationships that has made them feel as if they are living in a house full of strangers. There is an especially sharp sort of loneliness experienced only by those women who lie next to a man at night who doesn't know the Christ they know in a personal way. There is social loneliness—the "I'm left out all the time" feeling or "I'm never invited anymore" syndrome. There is also the loneliness of leadership to cope with. I'm sure I do not need to convince any reader of the fact of loneliness in people's experience today. You may be lonely yourself.

Perhaps above all is the loneliness of bereavement—the widow's agony. The finality of a closed coffin, a wardrobe of helpless-looking suits with no one to wear them anymore. The empty chair at the table or the fireside. We can see a God in Scripture who demonstrates His special compassion and care for such loneliness. The Old Testament gives witness to laws written by Moses concerning the care and protection of widows. The message of Scripture is persuasive and sober—"He defends the cause of the fatherless and widow" (Deut. 10:18, NIV). When we come to the New Testament, Jesus colors His teachings with illustrations and stories of widows in need and draws attention to a poor widow whom He commends for casting her "all" into the treasury (Mark 12:44). But it is in the story of the widow of Nain that we catch a glimpse of Christ's heart for the widow and also glean some practical help concerning the ways we can follow in His steps and meet some very great needs around us. The story is given in Luke 7:11-15, and you may want to pause at this point and read it.

Notice that the man who was deceased was the "only" son of his mother and she was a widow! "Double death" had snatched a woman's heart and life away. Christ stopped the funeral procession to tell her that He cared about her in that desperate situation. His Father in heaven understood about losing only sons! Next, Jesus commanded her not to weep. Then He created a reason for such an astonishing command. He delivered the child from death and presented him to his mother. Her loneliness had been but a temporary necessity, and reunion and rejoicing would now become the order of the day.

What joy is ours to be ambassadors for the Christ of hope to the widow! We can take the King's message to those who mourn. Christ still raises the dead! It may not be until the other side of death, but He promises to present our loved ones to us one fine day so that we can be with each other in the joy of an eternal togetherness. Faith enables us to anticipate that. First Thessalonians 4:16-17 tells us that Christ will bring those who have gone to heaven before us with Him when He returns again to earth. I can just see those who have gone before, crowding around Jesus as He is about to leave heaven. I can hear them saying, "Hurry back with our loved ones—we can hardly wait!" I can almost see Jesus' face and hear Him say, "Come with Me!" "So," says the Apostle Paul, "God will bring with Him those who sleep in Jesus" (1 Thes. 4:14, NKJV). "Then we who are alive and remain shall be caught up together with them in the clouds to meet the Lord in the air. And thus we shall always be with the Lord. Therefore comfort one another with these words" (1 Thes. 4:17-18, NKJV). God cares for sorrowing women and promises that one day the sorrow of loneliness will pass away forever (Rev. 21:4). That is worth stopping the funeral procession for and encouraging the mourners to weep not!

God understands the sorrow of rejection too. He has experienced rejection Himself and talks of His Son as "the stone which the builders rejected" (Matt. 21:42). Again, Isaiah tells us the Son of sorrows will be "despised and rejected of men" (Isa. 53:3). Read Matthew 15:21-28 and watch how our Lord lovingly ministers to a woman who experienced the bitterness of rejection.

Here was a woman who had sought out Christ because she perceived His love—even for outcasts and foreigners like herself. She was a woman of Canaan, despised by the Jews. Maybe you can identify with her. Have you ever been rejected because of the color of your skin, your culture, perhaps the way you dress, or even the way you talk? This woman was *apparently* even rejected by Christ Himself. Listen to the hard words He used. "Then she came and worshiped Him, saying, 'Lord, help me!' But He answered and said, 'It is not good to take the children's bread and throw it to the little dogs' " (Matt. 15:25-26, NKJV). At first He had refused to talk to her (v. 23) and His disciples had asked Him to send her away to stop her crying after them. She was being a nuisance! There is nothing that hurts more than feeling you are a nuisance. That's rejection.

But we are dealing with a woman of faith and persistence. God loved her! She would believe it to the end, even though Jesus would not speak to her. She would persist in her beliefs that He cared even when He broke His silence and used such harsh words—even when He seemed not to care at all! She reminds me of Jacob of old who wrestled with God and said, "I will not let You go unless You bless me!" (Gen. 32:26, NKJV) At last, Jesus smiled. He loves such trust and faith and delights to see it unshaken though tried! "O woman, great is your faith! Let it be to you as you desire" (Matt. 15:28, NKJV), He said to her, and the woman returned to a beloved daughter who had been possessed by demonic power and yet now was returned to her sanity and her mother's arms. She had been healed by a Christ who cared! (v. 28) As we think further of these examples of Jesus ministering to sorrowing women, perhaps you would like to borrow my prayer, bringing to mind the friends you know who sorrow without hope.

> Tender Jesus, caring for the ones who
>     care not anymore—
> For those beaten by circumstances
>     and driven by sorrow
>       to believe
>       they are lower than dogs,
> bereft of a reason to live.

Tender Jesus, moved with compassion
    for the sorrowing—
Meet us in our tears,
    dry our eyes and
    show us our duty:
Service that chases loneliness into the bosom
    of His love.

Tender Jesus, teach us the perseverance
    of prayer in the face of a
    silent heaven.

See us—women in Your life—
    sorrowing women who would
      see You smile
      feel Your hand of blessing
    touching awake faith in a Father who cares,
A Father who will never reject us.

Thank You, God,
    Thank You, Jesus,
      Thank You, Holy Spirit,
      for Your love.

# •TALKING IT OVER•

1. DISCUSS.                                                    *10 minutes*

☐ What did you learn about the source of sorrow?

☐ What did you learn about the Son of sorrow?
(See Hebrews 4:14-16.)

☐ Why are people lonely? Do you ever get lonely?

☐ What did the story of the widow of Nain teach
you? (Luke 7:11-15)

2. READ AND SHARE.                                            *15 minutes*

☐ Divide into twos and look up the verses below.
What encouragement do they give you? Talk
together or share with the whole group.

Deuteronomy 31:8        Mark 1:35
Psalm 68:6              Luke 5:16
Matthew 14:13           Acts 18:9-10
Matthew 28:20

☐ Review Matthew 15:21-28. If you were talking
to someone experiencing rejection, what one
thing would you say? Why?

3. PRAY.                                                       *5 minutes*
Pray for lonely and rejected people you know.

# •PRAYING IT THROUGH•

*Suggested Times*

1. Read Isaiah 53. Choose one verse about Christ's sufferings. Read it over three times. Shut your eyes and "see" it in your mind's eye.

   *3 minutes*

2. Praise God for His sufferings on your behalf. Use verses from Isaiah 53 if they help.

   *3 minutes*

3. Make lists under the following headings and pray for the people you have listed: *lonely people* (e.g., refugees), *rejected people* (e.g., my next-door neighbor left by his wife with two toddlers), *widows* (e.g., the old people in our church who don't feel needed anymore).

   *10 minutes*

4. Pray for yourself that God will meet your needs and use you to minister to hurting people. Borrow the prayer at the end of Food for Thought to closewith.

   *4 minutes*

# •DIGGING DEEPER•

1. One of the sources of sorrow in the world is Satan. Read Revelation 20:10. The *New Scofield Reference Bible* (C.I. Scofield, ed., Oxford University Press) has notes following this verse which give some background on Satan and his power. Most of the text of these notes is reprinted here for you. Read through them and also read the Scripture references and you will get a good idea of how powerful Satan is.

Note from the *New Scofield Reference Bible:*

> Satan, Summary: This fearful being, apparently created one of the cherubim . . . and anointed for a position of great authority, perhaps over the primitive creation ( . . . Ezek. 28:11-15), fell through pride (Isa. 14:12-14). His "I will" (Isa. 14:13) marks the introduction of sin into the universe. Cast out of heaven (Lk. 10:18), he makes earth and air the scene of his tireless activity (Eph. 2:2; 1 Peter 5:8). After the creation of man he entered into the serpent . . . and, beguiling Eve by his subtlety, secured the downfall of Adam and through him of the race, and the entrance of sin into the world of men (Rom. 5:12-14). The Adamic Covenant . . . promised the ultimate defeat of Satan through the "seed of the woman." Then began Satan's long warfare against the work of God on behalf of humanity, which still continues. The present world system (Rev. 13:8), organized upon the principles of force, greed, selfishness, ambition, and sinful pleasure, is his work and was the bribe which he offered to Christ (Mt. 4:8-9). Of that world system he is prince (John 14:30; 16:11), and god (2 Cor. 4:4). As "prince of the power of the air" (Eph. 2:2) he is at the head of a vast host of demons. . . . To him, under God, was committed upon earth the power of death (Heb. 2:14). Cast out of heaven as his proper sphere and "first estate," he still has access to God as the "accuser of the brethren" (Rev. 12:10) and is permitted a certain power of sifting or testing the self-confident and carnal among believers (Job 1:6-11; Lk. 22:31-32; 1 Cor. 5:5;

1 Tim. 1:20); but this is a strictly permissive and limited power, and believers so sifted are kept in faith through the advocacy of Christ (Lk. 22:31-32). . . . Defeated . . . , he will be cast into the lake of fire, his final doom. The notion that he reigns in hell is not Biblical. He is prince of this present world system but will be tormented in the lake of fire.

2. What is Satan's fate?
   Hebrews 2:14

   Revelation 20:10

3. What will the Lord one day do with sorrow?
   Isaiah 25:8

   Revelation 21:3-4

4. Read John 11:33-36. How can this be a comfort to Christians who are sorrowing?

5. Read 1 Kings 17:8-16 and 2 Kings 4:1-7. What did God do in these two passages to show He is concerned about widows?
   1 Kings 17:8-16

   2 Kings 4:1-7

6. One of the reasons Israel was punished by God was their mistreatment of widows. See Isaiah 10:1-6 and Malachi 3:5. We have a responsibility to help lonely people. Working in pairs, read the

following verses and answer the questions.

Psalm 68:5-6
Of what should we remind lonely people?

Isaiah 1:17
What should we do for lonely people, such as widows?

Titus 2:3-4
What should older women be encouraged to do?

7. Read the story of Leah and Rachel and Jacob in Genesis 29–30. List the reasons Leah was rejected by Jacob and Rachel.

8. What did God do to show Leah He was concerned about her? (Gen. 29:31-35; 30:17, 19, 21)

9. Read Hosea 11. How can this be a comfort to someone who feels rejected?

10. In pairs (with a partner different from the one you had for question 6) read one of the following passages:

Acts 14:1-2, 19
Acts 17:1-10
2 Corinthians 11:23-28

What are some things that happened to Paul that could have left him feeling lonely or rejected?

11. Read 2 Corinthians 4:8-11. What was Paul's response to loneliness and rejection?

12. What are some reasons we might reject someone?

13. Think of someone you have rejected by your words or actions. Ask God to help you love that person. What specific things can you do to show your love for that person?

# •TOOL CHEST•
*(A Suggested Optional Resource)*

*REFERENCE BIBLES*
There is a wide variety of reference or study Bibles available in many different translations. Some of them are:

| | | |
|---|---|---|
| *Open Bible* | in | *King James Version* (KJV) or *New American Standard* (NASB) |
| *Harper Study Bible* | in | *Revised Standard Version* (RSV) |
| *NIV Study Bible* | in | *New International Version* (NIV) |
| *Thompson Chain-Reference Bible* | in | KJV NIV |
| *Oxford Study Edition* | in | *New English Bible* (NEB) |
| *Ryrie Study Bible* | in | KJV, NASB |

A reference Bible contains the Scripture text, plus a combination of the following:

- a system of cross-references which direct the reader to other verses on the same topic
- a concordance
- maps
- explanatory footnotes
- introductions to each book
- outlines of books
- indexes
- suggestions on how to study the Bible

The price for a study Bible can be anywhere from $20 up, depending on the type of cover and paper.

The reference Bible featured in this lesson is the *New Scofield Reference Bible*, in the *King James Version*. A new edition is available in the *New International Version*, called the *Oxford NIV Scofield Study Bible*. Both contain extensive, helpful footnotes, such as the notes on Satan. The note included in this lesson is just one sample of the interesting and helpful information found in the *New Scofield Reference Bible* (C.I. Scofield, ed., Oxford University Press).

# 3

# Sick Women

Do you ever hear people saying things like, "I prayed my husband would get better, but I must be very wicked, since he died! Maybe I didn't have enough faith. . . ."Or, "healing happened in Christ's day, but that's because the people didn't have hospitals. . . ."Or, "I don't believe in miracles. . . ." What answer do we give when such questions arise?

The Bible reveals a God who visited a suffering world to address the problem of pain. God is wholeness. He is perfect health. There is no chaos or disorder in His whole being. He revealed Himself to His people in Israel as Jehovah *rapha*, the Lord who heals (Ex. 15:26). He assured His children He had the power to sustain healthy bodies and promised His life-giving energy to work in earthly matter so susceptible to germs and disease.

Satan is the source of sin and therefore of sickness. We live in a sin-sick creation that is dying, "groaning" as the Apostle Paul puts it, waiting for its redemption (Rom. 8:22).

So God is health and Satan is sickness. What havoc Lucifer has brought about! And yet, Christ restores. He died to bring us back from destruction, and He rose again for our justification. Now He lives in the power of an endless life. It is *this life* the believer can receive. Eternal life is the life of the Eternal One—a life that is healthy and does not disintegrate. It is self-sustaining life.

As Jesus of Nazareth began His earthly ministry, He claimed that He was God. He said that many things witnessed to the fact of His deity. In John 7, He pointed out to His enemies that He knew God and was God. "At this," the Scripture says, "they tried to seize Him. . . . Still, many in the crowd put their faith in Him. They said, 'When the Christ comes, will He do more miraculous signs than this man?' " (John 7:30-31, NIV) In another place Christ urged the people to believe what He said because His wonderful "works" declared His words to be authentic (John 10:37-38).

There are three words that generally go together in the Bible when we read about miracles. They are *miracles, signs,* and *wonders.* The *miracle* is the divine action in the incident. The *sign* speaks of the significance of the event, that is, the proof of Deity at work or the encouragement of faith to a doubting disciple. The *wonder* gives us the flavor of the reactions of the onlookers.

But we need to ask ourselves exactly what miracles are. Many in modern days doubt that such phenomena exist. Some admit that God *can* work miracles, but doubt that He *will.* C.S. Lewis says that when Jesus, as God incarnate, performed a miracle, He simply took the laws of nature that He Himself had instituted and reproduced a natural act at a different speed and on a smaller scale. "The miracles in fact are a retelling in small letters of the very same story which is written across the whole world in letters too large for some of us to see" ("Miracles," *God in the Dock*, Eerdmans, p. 29). In other words, *normal* is miracle. When God enables the vine to draw water into itself and produce juice that ferments, water is turned into wine. It is therefore a small thing for the same God in human form to accelerate the process at the wedding at Cana in Galilee. There in small letters the Incarnate One did what He has been doing ever since the days of Noah! As Lewis says, "some of the miracles do locally what God has already done universally. . . . At Cana the mask is off. The Son will do nothing but what He sees the Father do. There is, so to speak, a family *style*" ("Miracles," pp. 29-30).

I love these thoughts. Jesus is not a magic man. He works with His own natural laws because He stands beyond and outside them.

Think a while and realize that normal is indeed miracle. The larger letters that are too large for us to read are the things we take for granted every day of our lives; they are miracles in themselves.

"Normal" health is miracle! The body temperature that is kept at just the right heat through the functions of the skin, the renewal that goes on while we sleep, and even the fact that we wake up in the morning are all miracles! The miles of nervous system within us boggle the mind. That our hearts pump 220 gallons of blood per hour and that our noses stop growing seem small things because we never give them a serious thought. But I assure you it would *not* be a small thing if our noses didn't stop growing! It's *all* miracle. But these letters are too large for us to see.

The healing process itself is a miracle, like the slow, "normal" healing we all experience when we have a common cold. The doctor will tell us—there is no magic in the medicine we take. The medication can only stimulate nature's functions or remove hindrances to the body's revitalizing agents. No dressing will make a scar form over a cut upon a corpse. That needs the life of God, who is the life source of our very existence. This mysterious energy called life that works against death and disintegration comes from Him.

We have a good friend who is a surgeon. He teaches in a medical college and begins his lectures to his students with the words, "Gentlemen, we cut; God heals!" As we look at three miraculous things that Jesus did for women, we can see God doing locally in small letters the things He has been doing since the beginning of time in large ones.

In Mark 5:25-29 we read about a woman suffering from a debilitating physical condition. She, the Bible says, had tried everything but was in fact worse rather than better. Then Jesus touched her and "immediately" she was healed. Twenty-seven times in the Gospels we read about rapid miracles rather than slow ones.

In Luke 13:11-13 we read about a daughter of Abraham who had been bent over for eighteen years and could not straighten up at all. "Immediately" Jesus healed her. In Luke 8:1-3 we are told about many women who had been mentally or spiritually oppressed. Jesus cast demons out of some and healed the bodies and minds of others.

Yet the deepest and most significant miracle of all is that which has to do with the healing of the soul. Soul healing is by far the most important healing of all! In Luke 7:36-50 we meet a lady who had her sins forgiven by the Saviour. Her soul was sick, and Jesus saved it! He healed the eternal part of her. To heal a person's soul and make it whole enough for heaven is far and away the most miraculous healing of all!

God is the healer of bodies, souls, spirits, characters, and relationships. Satan can mend inanimate matter but he cannot bring peace of mind or mend sick marriages or cast out demons, for after all, how can Satan cast out Satan? "So who qualifies for healing?" you may ask. "Those who have enough faith? Those who are good enough? Does it depend on me or on Him? Is He choosy? Does He draw our names out of a hat? Is it just potluck?"

First of all, *all* who come to God for soul healing, asking in faith to be saved, will receive it. He is "not willing that *any* should perish but that *all* should come to repentance" (2 Peter 3:9, emphasis added). As we read in 1 John 5:11-12, "And this is the testimony: that God has given us eternal life, and this life is in His Son. He who has the Son has life; he who does not have the Son of God does not have life."

Some who ask for temporary bodily healing will receive it too. But not all who ask will. All of us will enjoy a final healing of the body in heaven. We shall receive, according to 1 Corinthians 15:35-54, a brand-new body which will never feel pain or experience decay! Certainly we may ask God to restore our bodies now while we are still on earth, when the occasion demands it. However, we *must* remember that all whom Jesus healed eventually died! We need to make sure we keep temporary bodily healing in perspective. Sometimes God will say yes to our prayers, and sometimes He will say no. Paul asked for healing and God said no to him. He gave him reasons, and in the end, Paul stopped asking to be made well (2 Cor. 12:7-10). God promised Paul the miracle of His sufficiency in the midst of an adversity He did not remove.

"Should I ask for healing?" I am so often asked. Yes, yes! But accept God's no if and when it comes. On the other hand, if God answers your prayers and you are raised from a bed of sickness, make sure you use your gift of new health to serve Him. When Jesus healed Peter's mother-in-law, she got up and ministered to them (Luke 4:39). A pastor friend of mine always asks this question of those who come to him for the prayer of healing according to James chapter 5. "What will you do with your life if He *does* heal you? Will you live it for Him or for yourself?" That is a vital question!

# •TALKING IT OVER•

---

1. DISCUSS. — *10 minutes*
   - ☐ What did you learn about miracles today that you didn't know before?
   - ☐ Can Satan heal?
   - ☐ How would you define health?
   - ☐ How should we pray for the sick?

---

2. READ AND SHARE. — *15 minutes*
   - ☐ Look up James 5:13-18 and 2 Corinthians 12:7-10. How can you reconcile these two passages?
   - ☐ Divide into twos. Each pair should read an instance of Jesus dealing with a sick woman: Matthew 9:20-22; Luke 13:11-13; Luke 7:36-50. Discuss the passage together and come up with one thing about healing that is meaningful to you. Share with the group.

---

3. PRAY. — *5 minutes*

Close in silent prayer for the sick in body and soul.

# •PRAYING IT THROUGH•

*Suggested
Times*

1. Read any portion of Isaiah 53. Praise God for His grace in sending us Christ.      *5 minutes*
2. Spend a few moments in intercessory prayer.      *8 minutes*
   - ☐ Pray by first name only for physically sick people you know.
   - ☐ Pray by first name only for depressed people you know.
   - ☐ Pray by first name only for spiritually sick (lost) people you know.

3. Read 2 Corinthians 12:7-10.      *3 minutes*
   - ☐ Pray for people who have not been healed yet. Pray that the Helper will comfort and console them.
   - ☐ Make a list of those people who have been mentioned by the group. Pray for them every day this week.

4. Discuss briefly one thing you can do to use your health for the Lord this week. Pray about it.      *4 minutes*

# •DIGGING DEEPER•

Read 1 Corinthians 15.

1. How can we know that the resurrection of Christ was not a hoax? List five reasons from 1 Corinthians 15:1-8.

2. Why is it important that the resurrection of Christ is not a hoax? (vv. 12-19)

3. What is the sequence of events of the resurrection of the dead? (vv. 21-28)

4. In verses 20 and 23, what does it mean that Christ is the firstfruits of the dead? What are the firstfruits? (Lev. 23:10) What is the significance of Christ being the firstfruits of the dead? If you are not familiar with the concept of firstfruits, you may want to look up these verses in a commentary on 1 Corinthians 15. Here is an excerpt from *An Exposition of the First Epistle to the Corinthians*, by Charles Hodge (Baker Book House, p. 323).

"The apostle does not mean merely that the resurrection of Christ was to precede that of His people; but as the first sheaf of the harvest presented to God as a thank-offering was a pledge and assurance of the ingathering of the whole harvest, so the resurrection of Christ is a pledge and proof of the resurrection of His people." Now can you answer the above questions?

5. In verses 35-49, what do we learn about resurrected bodies? How will our resurrected bodies differ from our earthly bodies?

6. How could you use 1 Corinthians 15 to encourage someone who is sick?

7. What difference does it make in your life that Jesus Christ rose from the dead? How have your attitudes and behavior changed as a result of the knowledge of the resurrection? Are there any changes you need to make as a result of this study?

# •TOOL CHEST•
*(A Suggested Optional Resource)*

### BIBLE COMMENTARIES
Bible commentaries are a supplement to, not a replacement for, a thorough study of Scripture. After you have read through a passage, studied it thoroughly, and drawn your own conclusions, then it is time to consult a commentary to clarify unclear passages or to get supplementary information.

There are commentaries available that cover the entire Bible. Other commentaries devote an entire volume to one individual book of the Bible. Many commentaries give a verse-by-verse explanation of the passage, as well as information on the meaning of words in the original language.

An important thing to remember when using commentaries is that they may be biased according to the author's point of view. Some commentators are better than others at presenting all the possible views on a given issue. Remember that the commentaries are not the authority—the Bible is.

Two good single commentaries on the whole Bible are *Matthew Henry's Commentary on the Whole Bible* (Zondervan) and *Wycliffe Bible Commentary* (Moody Press).

There are a number of sets of commentaries containing single volumes on individual books by different authors. Generally, the following sets are good:

*Expositor's Bible Commentary* (Zondervan) This is a fairly new set; at this time only the New Testament is completed. The Old Testament volumes are still being written.

*Tyndale Commentaries on the Old Testament* (InterVarsity Press)

*Tyndale Commentaries on the New Testament* (Eerdmans)

*Everyman's Bible Commentary* (Moody Press)

From an economic standpoint, it might be best to purchase a single-volume commentary on the whole Bible. If you desire to consult single volumes on individual books, it might be best to borrow them from a library or from an individual who has an extensive library, as these volumes tend to be expensive. It is a good idea to borrow and use a commentary before you buy it. But remember, do all your basic Scripture study *before* consulting a commentary.

# 4

# *Sensual Women*

## •FOOD FOR THOUGHT•

Let's talk about "the love lie." The love lie says that erotic love is the most important of the loves. It's the "feeling that is too big for words" love. "If it feels so good, it must be right," the teenager argues as she faces the issue of the boyfriend who wants her to go "too far" in their lovemaking. The problem with our society at the present time is that Eros has become God. People worship the sensual, sexual side of love and obey its desires.

Once my husband was speaking at a university campus. A young man joined the crowd and began to heckle him. "You Christians make me tired," he said somewhat belligerently. "Who says it's wrong to enjoy my sexuality? Society tells me it's OK to love as I please, as long as I don't hurt society." My husband pointed out that the young man had the capacity to populate a small village, and society would start caring in a hurry if every male lived up to his sexual capacity! He also explained that the young man may well feel good populating the small village, but a good feeling doesn't necessarily mean a good thing. Appetites must be controlled or we will destroy ourselves and others too.

The Bible is pretty explicit when it comes down to talking about sex. It tells us there are rules made by a God of love. God's love is primarily concerned with the loved ones' well-being. It desires the best and goes beyond itself to see that the best is given. Lust asks "what can I get?" while love inquires "what can I give?" Eros must be submitted to Agape, who will control it and keep it untainted. The marriage bond provides the arena for its glad expression. God protects sex by building marriage walls around it, not to keep enjoyment out, but rather to keep fulfillment in. Hebrews 13:4 tells us that marriage is honorable and chastity should be respected. It also tells us that God will judge those who traffic in the bodies of others or defile the relationship of marriage! Sex is protected by a loving God who thought of it in the first place and desires only the full enjoyment of a wonderful part of love within the context of the whole marriage relationship.

If there are rules, then they can be broken. I sometimes wonder if the world is not full of people racking their brains trying to beat the system! There is something within each and every one of us that says, "If you dare to lay down a rule on me, I'll break it over your head!" The rules of love are broken continually, and the Bible says that God will judge those who break them. But notice—God is the judge. I am not to be the one that decides who is and who is not guilty. In fact, after laying out a pretty graphic picture of sin in Romans 1, Paul immediately warns us against a condemning attitude toward sinners, since we are all sinners and are therefore all guilty (Rom. 2:1-2). Nowhere is this better exemplified than in the life of the Lord Jesus, who came face to face with sexual sin and dealt with it in a manner that gives us cause for both hope and caution.

The rules of love were laid down by one who came to love us even unto death. He portrayed a life of love based not on feelings but rather on a commitment made before the world began—a commitment the Trinity made to love a lost world back to God.

We have three instances of love in human form in the shape of Jesus Christ as He met women whose lives had fallen apart. These women had worshiped Eros and had found him a stern, destructive master, tearing apart their relationships, damaging their reputations, and bringing grief to themselves and everyone around them.

First let's look at Jesus and the woman at the well in John 4. Jesus took the short route from Galilee to Jerusalem even though it passed right through Samaria. Jews normally had no dealings with the Samaritans; their bitterness and hostility had its roots in the Old Testament times. The Jews said, "He who eats the bread of Samaritans is he who eats sinner's flesh!" They also said, "No Samaritan shall be made a proselyte" and "they have no share in the resurrection of the dead." Jesus, however, spoke well of them (Luke 10:30-37). He rebuked His disciples for wanting to call down fire and burn them up (Luke 9:55-56), healed a Samaritan leper, and gave us one of the most tender memories of His life lived among us in the account of His dealings with the Samaritan woman at the well of Sychar.

Jesus, though weary with His journey, was in no wise weary of His work, and He spent His resting moments at the well explaining His presence there. Offering the woman who had come to draw water an alternative to her insatiable thirst for satisfaction (evidenced in five marriages and the live-in arrangement of the moment), Jesus had the great joy of watching her leave her bucket—a symbol of her constant thirst. Then she ran back to the men in her village to urge them to come meet the Christ! (John 4:28-29) In the words of Herbert Lockyer, "at Jacob's well she saw Jacob's Star . . . and ascending Jacob's Ladder . . . became the means of others climbing to God" (*All the Women of the Bible*, Zondervan, p. 239).

Next we see the Lord of love facing a sticky moment in the temple courtyard (John 8:1-11). His teaching had been rudely interrupted by the arrival of the Pharisees dragging a woman snatched literally from the bed of adultery—"in the very act," as one of the pious men announced triumphantly. The Pharisees were ever eager to deal with harlots. They considered themselves custodians of public morality, treating "sinners" with sanctimonious contempt. Even though according to the law, both parties to the act of adultery should have been brought to judgment (Lev. 20:10), only the woman appeared. Eager to cast the first stone, they baited Christ, seeking to entrap Him. If He allowed the woman to go free He could be shown to despise the law. No concern or thought was given to the woman, who, exposed, ashamed, and no doubt frightened for her life, stood in the midst of the hostile crowd.

But Jesus did not allow one of them to cast a stone. In fact, He used wise words to "stone the cast" of hypocritical actors on the stage! "He who is without sin among you, let him throw a stone at her first," He said. Well, that went down like a ham sandwich in a synagogue, as the saying goes! From the oldest to the youngest, the men slunk away, and the crowd also disappeared in the face of such wisdom. The woman left alone heard Judge Jesus pass sentence. "Neither do I condemn you; go and sin no more."

In Luke 7 we have the story of a woman who was a well-known sinner. She found the Lord Jesus eating a meal, and kneeling at His feet, washed them with tears of repentance and wiped them with her hair. Thus, she gave to Him the courtesy and honor due to a guest in the East. The woman who had once worshiped Eros worshiped Agape Himself, and so found herself pardoned and at peace.

How can we apply the lessons of this study? So often when faced with a sexual mode of conduct that contradicts our own standard of Christian behavior, we fail to speak out. It's hard, isn't it? A friend of mine grappled with the problem of what to do about her daughter who was living with her boyfriend at college. The girl asked if she could bring the young man home for the weekend and let her parents know they expected to sleep together. "We'll use my room, Mom," the girl said breezily!

"We want to keep the lines of communication open," my friend said, "but we don't approve of what they are doing." I suggested that they welcome the young couple home but tell them very firmly that they would not be sleeping together under their roof! We have to show acceptance of the person without an acceptance of their sin.

Jesus demonstrated love and understanding. He allowed sinners to touch Him (something Pharisees would *never* allow) and Himself touched the souls of desperately needy women, bringing the satisfaction of righteousness into their lives.

In the end, we must not have a spirit of condemnation, for after all, He is the Judge—not we. He alone knows the circumstances and pressures of people's lives and why they have succumbed to temptation. Our part is to leave the judging to Him. At the same time we can let our feelings and beliefs be known and expect change. It is quite all right to say to our children, "go and sin no more" and to point out that adultery *is* adultery, perversion *is* perversion, and homosexuality is, according to Scripture, a sexual choice and one that God condemns. The most important thing is to remember not to condemn, but rather to proclaim the difference between right and wrong and offer the water of life, the pardon of God, and the joy of the Saviour to any we can get to listen to us!

# •TALKING IT OVER•

1. DEFINE.                                          *2 minutes*
   ☐ Agape love
   ☐ Eros love

2. READ AND SHARE.                          *15 minutes*
   ☐ Read Romans 1:18-32. Choose a verse you
     would like to make headlines in *USA Today*.
     Say why.
   ☐ In twos take one of the three stories below and
     write down one thing you can learn from Jesus,
     one thing you can learn from the woman, and
     one thing you can learn from the crowd. Share
     with the whole group. John 4:1-42 (the woman
     at the well); John 8:1-12 (the woman taken in
     adultery); Luke 7:36-50 (the woman in the
     Pharisee's house).

3. REVIEW.                                          *10 minutes*
   Which part of the application of the lesson do you
   need to pray about and why?
   ☐ Love as He loved.
   ☐ Live as He lived.
   ☐ Don't condemn.
   ☐ Expect change.

4. PRAY.                                            *3 minutes*

# •PRAYING IT THROUGH•

*Suggested Times*

1. Praise God for His attributes.    *5 minutes*
   - ☐ His holiness and purity
   - ☐ His grace and forgiveness
   - ☐ His love and compassion

2. Pray for these people.    *10 minutes*
   - ☐ People tempted to commit adultery
   - ☐ Teenagers tempted to worship Eros
   - ☐ Your church's youth group
   - ☐ Parents struggling to relate to their children, grandchildren, and families

3. Pray silently.    *5 minutes*
   - ☐ Examine your own heart.
   - ☐ Confess any condemning attitudes.
   - ☐ Ask God what needs to change in your own life.

# •DIGGING DEEPER•

1. Why did God institute marriage?
   Genesis 2:18

   1 Corinthians 7:1-9

   Ephesians 5:22-33

2. What is the proper setting for sexual expression?
   Genesis 2:24

   Hebrews 13:4

3. What restrictions has God put on our sexuality?
   Deuteronomy 5:18

   Matthew 5:27-28

   1 Corinthians 6:15-16

   1 Thessalonians 4:3-7

4. Why has God set these definite limits on how we may use our sexuality?



5. What is the outcome of an immoral lifestyle?
   Proverbs 7:6-27

   Galatians 5:19-21

   Ephesians 5:5

   Colossians 3:5-6

6. Look up marriage in a Bible dictionary. Read the whole section, then read specifically any sections that cover the topic of polygamy. The following paragraphs are from *The New Bible Dictionary* (second edition) published by Tyndale (pp. 742-743).

> Monogamy is implicit in the story of Adam and Eve, since God created only one wife for Adam. Yet polygamy is adopted from the time of Lamech (Gen. 4:19), and is not forbidden in Scripture. It would seem that God left it to man to discover by experience that his original institution of monogamy was the proper relationship. It is shown that polygamy brings trouble, and often results in sin, e.g. Abraham (Gen. 21); Gideon (Jud. 8:29–9:57); David (2 Sam. 11:13); Solomon (1 Kings 11:1-8). In view of oriental customs Hebrew kings are warned against it (Deut. 17:17). Family jealousies arise from it, as with Elkanah's two wives, one of whom is an adversary to the other (1 Sam. 1:6; cf. Lev. 18:18). . . .
>
> When polygamy was practiced the status and relationship of the wives can be gathered both from the narratives and the law. It was natural that the husband would be drawn to one rather than another. Thus Jacob, who was tricked into polygamy, loved Rachel more than Leah (Gen. 29). Elkanah preferred Hannah in spite of her childlessness (1 Sam. 1:1-8). In Deut. 21:15-17 it is admitted that the husband may love one wife and hate the other.

7. Although polygamy was not the ideal God had in mind for marriage, it was at times practiced in the Old Testament. What are some problems polygamy can produce?
Genesis 29:30; 30:1


1 Samuel 1:4-7

8. What advice does Proverbs 5:15-21 give concerning sexuality?

   This advice was given to a man, but what principles can be drawn from it what would apply to a woman?

9. Whether you are married or single, what does God expect from you in terms of your sexuality, and what provisions has God given you to meet those expectations?

10. What obstacles would hinder you from maintaining this ideal?

    How can you handle these obstacles?

11. Write a prayer asking God to help you avoid sexual sins and live in a way that pleases Him.

# •TOOL CHEST•
*(A Suggested Optional Resource)*

### BIBLE DICTIONARIES
One of the most valuable Bible study tools available is the Bible dictionary. It is used in much the same way as an English language dictionary but contains much more information for most entries. To use such a tool you would only need to look up the word or subject in question, and the Bible dictionary will guide you from there. For instance, if you are reading about the church at Philadelphia in Revelation 3:7-13, it is essential to understand something about the city of Philadelphia to understand the passage. The description of the city vividly illuminates what Christ was saying to that church because the Lord used imagery that was familiar to those Philadelphian believers.

The Bible dictionary featured in this lesson was *The New Bible Dictionary* (second edition) published by Tyndale. It is a one-volume Bible dictionary. The exact text of this dictionary is included in the three-volume *Illustrated Bible Dictionary*, also published by Tyndale. This set is rich in colorful illustrations, graphs, and photographs which go along with the text.

So when you come to a word or subject you don't understand, or would like more information on a topic, consult your Bible dictionary.

# 5

# *Successful Women*

## •FOOD FOR THOUGHT•

Jesus had been preaching the Gospel in His own home area. Now He began to make a circuit of the cities and towns around Galilee, taking His little band of workers along. Luke 8:1-3 tells us that His disciples and many women traveled with Him.

Among the women were three who are singled out for us: Mary Magdalene, Joanna, and Susanna. We learn that they were women who were influential, wealthy, and of good reputation. They used their money and goods and all their talented energies to minister to Jesus and His team. Rabbis were not in the habit of allowing women to accompany them on their teaching tours. Jesus elevated the place of women by sharing His mission with them. They were in no way mere hangers-on. They were part of the Saviour's plan and purpose.

We tend to forget that thirteen hungry men would need breakfast, lunch, and dinner! They would have to have lodging for the night and daily necessities provided along the way. Out of their abundance, these "many" grateful women shared their earthly possessions with the group of travelers.

In every modern sense of the word, these women were successful. They probably had fancy homes, lovely clothes, and lots of money. They were popular and respected. And yet the Bible tells us that some were also stricken with various maladies that made all these things totally irrelevant. Money could not always buy the medicine to cure their sicknesses. Influence and popularity were soon forgotten when mental aberrations controlled their behavior. Jesus touched each need, healed them of all their diseases, and in gratitude they aligned themselves with His cause and served Him.

All women who serve Jesus are successful women as far as God is concerned. Perhaps two of the most famous are Mary and Martha. Most of us have heard about them! Let's think about Martha first.

Luke 10 tells us that "a woman named Martha opened her home to Him" (v. 38, NIV). Martha was undoubtedly wealthy, generous, and respected in the community. Jesus was by now a "wanted" man. Yet He was not arrested while He stayed under Martha's roof. He was safe there. Martha had met the Saviour at some point and had perhaps been with Him on one of His many missionary tours. We do not know for certain when she met the Lord or if she and her sister Mary were included in the band of women mentioned in Luke 8, but we do have the account of her excited hospitality as the disciples and Jesus arrived in town.

We catch a picture of this able woman, bustling about getting her servants organized and planning a feast for everybody. Nothing was too much trouble. She was, I'm sure, the "hostess with the mostest"! It all spelled hard work as hospitality always does, so it's not really surprising to find Martha getting irritated with her sister, whom she found sitting at Jesus' feet instead of giving her a helping hand! Which of us has not experienced such feelings? Who has not fumed at the family seated happily in front of the TV while we slaved away in the kitchen? I'm sure Martha was longing to sit at the feet of Jesus too, but she knew there were hungry men to feed.

I gather that Martha was an "overdoer." In fact, as H.V. Morton has said, Jesus uses a play on words when He lovingly rebukes her, saying in effect, "Martha, Martha, you are busy with many courses when one dish would be quite sufficient. Mary has chosen the best dish, which shall not be taken away from her."

How some of us can relate to that! Doers usually tend to overdo, just as sitters and dreamers can become lazy! In fact, our assets can become our liabilities.

People are always more important than preparations. Jesus knew He had very little time left on earth to talk to Mary and Martha. He had so many things to tell them that were far more important than eating a seven-course meal. For this reason, one course would have been quite sufficient. It was a question of priorities. Martha had been distracted by the very service she sought to render to her Saviour. And that is easy to do!

I love *doing.* I love serving Jesus. I love the details and the planning and the actual physical activity that is involved. I love having an open home like the one Martha had and having the world tramp through it. I enjoy cooking and getting the bedrooms ready. What joy to fill our lovely home with students or missionaries or people in need! Yet there have been many times when I have heard the Lord rebuke me too. I have become distracted from the Saviour by my very involvement. I have not taken time to sit at His feet and listen to His Word as Mary did.

Then, like Martha I find myself becoming disgruntled. I discover a sense of frustration inside me with the people around me, who do not appear to be doing nearly as much as I am! "They are not pulling their weight," I say to myself, and like Martha I usually voice my frustration to the Lord.

"Don't you care that my sisters have left me to serve alone?" I ask Him. Once you've been distracted, it's very easy to become disgruntled! The sense of frustration soon turns into a feeling of isolation, and you begin to believe you are the only one doing anything for Jesus!

Then it's not long before the frustration and sense of isolation result in irritation with everyone around you—even with the Lord Himself! You begin to feel lonely, put-upon, and hurt.

What's more, if there's one thing worse than planning a party that ends up planning you, it's being unappreciated by the guest of honor! For Martha, the whole affair culminated in a great black cloud. She became "worried and upset" (v. 41, NIV). In brief, she found herself in a frantic tizzy!

Jesus' gentle rebuke brought her back to basics. He thoroughly appreciated all her hard work, but first and foremost He wanted her to know He appreciated *her!* She was so much more important than anything she did for Him, and she needed to look into His face and remember that. Then her services would spring from a pure motivation and be rendered sweetly rather than sourly.

I have always been amazed to find out that the majority of women are Marthas. I suspect our menfolk think of all of us as Marys—reflective, pensive, quiet, mystical rather than practical. Yet, whenever I invite women to raise their hands to indicate with whom they identify better, Mary or Martha, the vast majority say "Martha"! For this reason, men ought not to presume we women are doing all the praying while they go about the preaching and the practical things of life; the praying is perhaps not being done at all! We Marthas need to listen to the Lord's rebuke, accept His correction, and leave our less necessary duties to do what is most necessary—spend time with Him. The rest will surely fall into place, and schedules will take care of themselves.

The last glimpse we have of Martha is in the house of a neighbor after the raising of Lazarus, her brother. Jesus is once again in town, and this time there are more guests than ever for supper. After all, there were plenty of people who wanted to see Lazarus as well as Jesus now! Mary was busy preparing her little alabaster box to give to Jesus, while Martha, the Bible tells us, "served" (John 12:2). What an epitaph! "Martha served"—there it is in all its stark simplicity. This time there is no rebuke from the Lord, no raw reaction of irritation from Martha, no record of wrong attitudes. Service, she now knew, must spring from a Christ-consciousness, and a Christ-consciousness comes from spending a few private moments with Him. Martha discovered that success is the smile of Christ on our endeavors, be it the work of prayer or the work of work. Now Martha was ready to work diligently and provide a feast for a King, her King—King Jesus. Martha had learned her lesson—I wonder if we have learned ours?

# •TALKING IT OVER•

*Suggested<br>Times*

1. BRAINSTORM.                          *10 minutes*
   Read Matthew 6:25-34 and make a list of the things from this passage that the world counts as symbols of success. What is Christ's recipe for successful living in these verses? Discuss.

2. READ AND SHARE.                   *8 minutes*
   ☐ Read Luke 10:38-42. Identify yourself. Are you a Martha or a Mary?
   ☐ What sort of people irritate you? Why do you think that is?
   ☐ Do you ever feel unappreciated?

3. DISCUSS.                              *10 minutes*
   ☐ How can we know if we have been "distracted" by our much serving?
   ☐ What do you think God wants to change about us—our personalities? our attitudes?
   ☐ If you could have a sentence about yourself written in the Bible, such as the one describing Martha in John 12:2, "Martha served," what would you want it to be? Share it with the group.

4. PRAY.                                    *2 minutes*

# •PRAYING IT THROUGH•

*Suggested Times*

1. Praise God for the benefits you have.      *5 minutes*
   - ☐ The material wealth you have been given
   - ☐ The influence God has given you
   - ☐ The home you live in
   - ☐ The freedom you enjoy
   - ☐ The training you have received

2. Pray silently about some of the symbols of success that are yours. Are you using them for the Lord?      *2 minutes*

3. Spend a few moments in intercessory prayer.      *10 minutes*
   - ☐ Pray for successful people you know who are entangled in their success. Pray that they will allow Jesus to set them free to serve Him.
   - ☐ Pray for Christians who are entrusted with great wealth that God will help them to be good stewards. Pray for yourselves that you will be able to administer your goods and property faithfully.
   - ☐ Pray for talented and spiritually successful people, who can so easily get "distracted" by all they're doing for God. Pray for prominent ministers, authors, singers, and missionaries.

4. Jesus told us that a "Mary attitude" is a matter of choice—"Mary has *chosen* what is better" (Luke 10:42, NIV). Spend the last few moments thinking about making that choice.      *3 minutes*

# •DIGGING DEEPER•

1. Wealth is one of the main symbols of success in our society today. Let's dig deeper into a biblical view of wealth. Look up the following verses and summarize what they have to say about wealth.

   | Reference | Summary |
   |---|---|
   | Deuteronomy 8:10-18 | Praise God for what He has given you and don't forget what He has done. |
   | Job 36:19 | |
   | Psalm 49:16-17 | |
   | Ecclesiastes 5:19 | |
   | Malachi 3:8-12 | |
   | Matthew 6:33 | |
   | Mark 10:23-25 | |
   | Luke 6:24 | |
   | Luke 12:16-21 | |
   | 1 Timothy 6:6-10 | |
   | 1 Timothy 6:17-19 | |
   | James 1:17 | |
   | James 5:1-6 | |

2. Categorize the references from question 1 under the appropriate headings by topic.
   Origin of wealth   Stewardship of wealth   Warnings about wealth

3. Write a short paragraph (three or four sentences) explaining what God's view is of the origins and stewardship of wealth and what are His warnings about wealth.

4. Look up *riches* in a concordance. The following list of verses containing the word *riches* is from Strong's *Exhaustive Concordance to the Bible*. Pick out one verse that you think is applicable to this lesson and summarize what the verse says. Decide into which category from question 2 this verse fits. Then do the same with the list of verses containing the word *wealth*, which is also from Strong's *Concordance*.

riches

| Isa. | 8: 4 | *r* of Damascus and the spoil of | 2428 |
|------|------|-----------------------------------|------|
|      | 10:14 | found as a nest the *r* of the people | " |
|      | 30: 6 | carry their *r* upon the shoulders of | " |
|      | 45: 3 | and hidden *r* of secret places, | 4301 |
|      | 61: 6 | ye shall eat the *r* of the Gentiles, | 2428 |
| Jer. | 9:23 | not the rich man glory in his *r:* | 6239 |
|      | 17:11 | he that getteth *r*, and not by right | " |
|      | 48:36 | *r* . . . he hath gotten are perished. | 3502 |
| Ezek. | 26:12 | they shall make a spoil of thy *r*, | 2428 |
|      | 27:12 | of the multitude of all kind of *r;* | 1952 |
|      | 18 | making, for the multitude of all *r;* | " |
|      | 27 | *r*, and thy fairs, thy merchandise, | " |
|      | 33 | earth with the multitude of thy *r* | " |
|      | 28: 4 | thou has gotten thee *r*, and hast | 2428 |
|      | 5 | traffick hast thou increased thy *r,* | " |
|      | 5 | heart is lifted up because of thy *r.* | " |

wealth

| Job | 21:13 | They spend their days in *w*, and in | 2896 |
|-----|-------|--------------------------------------|------|
|      | 31:25 | rejoiced because my *w* was great, | 2428 |
| Ps. | 44:12 | not increase thy *w* by their price | 2428 |
|      | 49: 6 | They that trust in their *w*, and | 2428 |
|      | 10 | perish, and leave their *w* to others | " |
|      | 112: 3 | ,W and riches . . . be in his house: | 1952 |
| Prov. | 5:10 | strangers be filled with thy *w;* | 3581 |
|      | 10:15 | rich man's *w* is his strong city: | 1952 |
|      | 13:11 | *W* gotten by vanity shall be | " |
|      | 22 | the *w* of the sinner is laid up for | 2428 |
|      | 18:11 | rich man's *w* is his strong city, | 1952 |
|      | 19: 4 | *W* maketh many friends; but the | " |

Summarize the verse on *riches:*

Into which category in question 2 would this verse fit?

Summarize the verse on *wealth:*

Into which category in question 2 would this verse fit?

5. Evaluate your stewardship. Are you practicing what God wants in terms of how you use what you have? In what ways are you falling short?

6. Which of God's warnings concerning wealth most applies to you? Why?

7. What one thing do you need to do to act out what you know about wealth? What hinders you from doing that?

# •TOOL CHEST•
*(A Suggested Optional Resource)*

## CONCORDANCES

A concordance is an invaluable tool for discovering what the Bible says about any topic you choose. It lists all the biblical references to a particular word in their order of appearance in the Bible. For example to find out what the Bible says about love, you would look up the word *love* in a concordance (the words are listed alphabetically) and read through the references listed there. The Scripture reference is given along with an excerpt from the verse that includes the word you have looked up (which is often identified by its first letter alone). Some concordances are *complete* (all the occurrences of all the most important terms, leaving out words like *the* and *and*); some are *exhaustive* (usually including even the *thes* and *ands!*); and some are simply listings of some of the major references to the most important words. The best concordances let you know in some way when the biblical writer has used different Hebrew, Aramaic, or Greek words so that you can differentiate between them; for instance, in the Bible there are numerous different words all translated by the English word *love*, and they do not all have the same shade of meaning. As always, the best thing to do is to work with several different concordances for a while and see which one is best for you before you buy one. Of course, the translation that you regularly use for study will influence your decision too, since each concordance is based on a particular English translation.

Concordances to the *King James Version:*
    Cruden, A.; *A Complete Concordance to the Bible.*
    Strong, J.; *An Exhaustive Concordance to the Bible*
    Young, R.; *An Analytical Concordance to the Bible.*
Concordance for the *New International Version:*
    Goodrick, E.W. and Kohlenberger, J.R.; *The NIV Complete Concordance.*
Concordance for the *New American Standard Bible:*
    Thomas, R.L.; *New American Standard Exhaustive Concordance of the Bible.*
Concordance for the *Revised Standard Version:*

Ellison, J.W.; *Nelson's Complete Concordance to the Revised Standard Version.*

The excerpts in this lesson are from *Strong's Exhaustive Concordance of the Bible.* The number at the end of each reference refers you to the Hebrew and Greek dictionaries in the back. For example, under *wealth*, Job 31:25, the number *2428* is given. Because it is an Old Testament verse, you would go to the Hebrew and Chaldee dictionary and look for *2428*. The Hebrew word used in that verse is given along with its meaning. If you look through the verses listed under *riches*, you'll notice some of them also have the number *2428*, telling you that the same Hebrew word was used in those verses as well. Words from the New Testament verses would be found in the Greek dictionary.

A concordance is a basic tool that should be a part of everyone's library, if possible.

# 6

# *Spiritual Women*

## •FOOD FOR THOUGHT•

Do spiritual women have halos around their heads, or are they real people? Did Mary of Bethany always have a religious bent, or was she like you and me—ordinary—until she met the extraordinary Christ? What makes a woman spiritual?

We don't know where Mary first met Christ. It could have been in Jerusalem at one of the feast days. It may be that she was introduced to Him by her sister, Martha. Perhaps she watched Him heal a leper or heard about His teachings from some of the other women who accompanied Him on His preaching tours. But even though we do not know *where* Mary first met Jesus, we can be absolutely sure she knew Him well—perhaps better than anyone else on earth.

To know *about* someone is not the same as knowing him personally. I knew all about Jesus Christ before I ever met Him. I had heard about His miracles from my Sunday School teacher and had learned to say set prayers from my earliest days. And yet He was not a reality in my life until I asked if I might know Him personally. What a difference that made! He had promised He would live within any who asked Him to, and I discovered the reality of that experience for myself (John 14:23). I no longer needed to borrow someone else's words in order to speak to Him; I could use my own. He had become my teacher and my friend, and I found myself sitting at His feet and listening to His Word just like Mary. Do *you* know Christ personally, or do you only know about Him? Are the facts you have gleaned about His sayings and His doings merely hearsay, or have you been to the source of those sayings and doings and asked your own questions?

The first time we meet Mary she is characteristically sitting attentively at her Lord's feet. We have already reviewed the incident through Martha's eyes. Mary's example, however, is important.

What does it take to choose the "good part," as the Lord Jesus called Mary's position? I believe it takes first of all a discerning spirit. Do we have the intelligence and sense to know what is important? We are subjected to such a barrage of advertising these days that we are almost brainwashed into believing that beer or beauty or our own bodies are the most important things in the world. Are we thinking hard enough to realize that alcohol can only give us a temporary lift, beauty is at best fleeting, and our bodies soon begin to need repair?

The body was in fact the issue in Martha's home the day Mary sat at Jesus' feet instead of preparing temporary relief for their hungry guests. She was discerning enough to know that "man shall not live by bread alone; but man lives by every word that proceeds out of the mouth of the Lord" (Deut. 8:3).

*Knowing* these things, however, isn't *doing* these things! That takes discipline. I'm sure Mary took every chance she had to listen to Christ. Do we? It takes lots of discipline to leave the necessary duties for the *most* necessary one.

Once I had the most disciplined of regimes. I would rise at the same time every day, and after dressing I would have an hour-long quiet time with the Lord. My schedule was a regulated one, and it was comparatively easy to create this happy habit and stick with it. Then I got married, and ten months later our firstborn son, David, arrived. My schedule lay in ruins! Every day was different. Trying to wake up before the baby was well-nigh impossible, and waiting until the baby was fed, burped, and slumbering again meant many a day went by without that blessed quiet with God I had come to rely on. I had to *really* learn the meaning of discipline.

Do we know how to leave the necessary for the *most* necessary things if and when we get the chance? Mary was able to do that, and what a delight it must have been to hear God's words from God's lips in human phrases she could understand! Wouldn't you love to know all the things Jesus said to Mary at those times? I would! And yet, though I cannot see Him with my eyes, I can go to Him in prayer, read His Word, and "hear" Him speaking to me today! That is sheer delight. So Mary was discerning, disciplined, and delighted to sit at the Lord's feet and listen to Him.

Perhaps we get the impression that Mary, knowing and loving Jesus as she did, never doubted Him at all. Yet her faith in Christ's love *was* shaken on at least one occasion, and I must admit that that gives me a little comfort! Mary, like Martha, had suffered from acute distress when Jesus, having received the message that their brother Lazarus was extremely ill, still stayed in the same place (John 11:6). He hadn't come when they called for Him, and Lazarus died. Struggling with her grief, Mary stayed in the house when Jesus eventually came. Did she stay there because she didn't want to see Him? We aren't told that, but it seems reasonable to me. It's hard to look into the face of someone who has disappointed you.

Jesus called for her and she came then, falling at His feet and repeating the identical words that Martha had uttered (although she had not been there to hear them). "If You had been here, my brother would not have died" (John 11:32). In other words she was saying, "Where were You when I needed You? Why, oh why, if You love us as You say You do, did You leave Lazarus to suffer so?"

I'm interested in the body language we see in the narrative. Like Martha, Mary knelt to issue her charge! How often I find myself in such a posture. I kneel at my bedside, looking as though I'm in submission to my Lord, but inside I'm unhappy and upset. Have you ever knelt to pray, looking and sounding right outwardly yet inwardly standing up tall and straight, almost shaking your fist in God's face?

We can see clearly the deep, deep love of Jesus in this story. When He did come to Bethany to teach the women the greater truth of His resurrection power, He didn't defend His actions or explain His absence. He saw their deep inexhaustible grief and, "groaning" in Himself, stood in front of Lazarus' tomb weeping. He wept for all the Marys and Marthas in the world who would experience death, when the stone of separation would be rolled between themselves and their loved ones. His tears tell us His heart (John 11:35). Lazarus—reluctantly I'm sure—returned from paradise to this cruel world to begin the death process all over again, and it was time for the sisters to rejoice in the reunion.

The next time we meet the sisters and Lazarus, another meal is being prepared under Martha's able supervision (John 12:1-8). Mary absents herself for a few moments to steal upstairs and fetch her little alabaster box of ointment, a very precious possession indeed. Knowing that this time Jesus had come to Jerusalem to die, and understanding Him well, Mary anoints His feet to prepare Him for His burial. It takes hours of listening and learning to discern God's will, and Mary had proved herself unique among the disciples in comprehending His predictions concerning His death. If we want to share in carrying out God's purposes, we will need to learn to be like Mary.

The little box intrigues me. It can represent so many things. For Mary herself it certainly represented a costly possession. The money that could have been generated by the sale of the perfume would have taken care of the needs of a single woman like herself. Some have said it was her marriage box, a provision for her future.

I well remember coming across this incident in my Bible reading at a time of great struggle in my life. My husband traveled widely, and it seemed to me that God was asking me for my "little box." At that moment it represented my marriage—a very precious possession. I knew I needed to pour out that gift upon Jesus in order that the fragrance of the sacrifice might fill my house. I realized that once I had given Him my little box, He would be glorified.

At other times the little box has represented other things for me. I have realized that the little box of time or the little box of money has not been yielded to God. What does the little box represent in your life? If in love you offer your little box willingly, what joy you will bring to His heart!

Mary's beautiful act of love was not appreciated by those that watched. It was considered unseemly and even downright wasteful by some who were there, but the Lord Jesus Christ appreciated it, and that is the most important thing.

Jesus loved Mary. He loved her because she was discerning, disciplined, and delighted with Him. He loved her through her periods of doubt and despair, and He loved her for her grand display of adoration as she poured upon Him her costliest sacrifice, putting her future in His hands.

I want to be like Mary—don't you? We have a choice about the matter. Mary *chose* the better part (Luke 10:42). So may we!

# •TALKING IT OVER•

---

1. SHARE.
   Share with the group how you met Christ. Keep it short—a few sentences will do. How much had you heard about Jesus before you met Him personally? Who introduced you?

   *8 minutes*

---

2. READ AND DISCUSS.
   Read John 12:1-11. What do you learn from these verses about each of the following?
   ☐ Jesus
   ☐ Lazarus
   ☐ Martha
   ☐ Judas
   ☐ The crowd
   ☐ The chief priests
   ☐ Mary

   *10 minutes*

---

3. SHARE.
   ☐ What does Mary's little box represent in your life?
   ☐ Starting anywhere you like in Psalm 119, read a few verses quietly to yourself and share what they teach you about the value of the Word of God.

   *10 minutes*

---

4. PRAY.
   Thank God for Mary's example.

   *2 minutes*

# •PRAYING IT THROUGH•

*Suggested
Times*

1. Pray about your quiet time.                                    *8 minutes*
   - ☐ Priorities
   - ☐ A more meaningful prayer time
   - ☐ Discipline
   - ☐ Distractions
   - ☐ Disappointments that may keep you from praying
   - ☐ That you may please God with your worship

2. Pray about your little boxes (if appropriate). (This    *5 minutes*
   can be silent time if the leader deems it
   necessary.)
   - ☐ Identify them in prayer.
   - ☐ Talk about them in prayer.
   - ☐ Yield them up in prayer.

3. Pray about your attitude. Three times Mary is    *7 minutes*
   found at Jesus' feet (Luke 10:39; John 11:32, John
   12:3).
   - ☐ Read the verses.
   - ☐ Meditate on them.
   - ☐ Pray about them.

## •DIGGING DEEPER•

1. Read Matthew 6:19-21. What are some examples of earthly treasures we should *not* store up?

2. What kinds of treasures *should* we be storing up? See Matthew 10:42, Matthew 25:34-40; 1 Timothy 6:17-19. Think of some other specific examples of ways to store up treasures in heaven.

3. Read Matthew 6:22-23. What do you think "the eye" means? Rewrite these two verses in your own words.

The metaphor of the eye in a moral sense was quite common among the Jews. A good eye signified a generous soul, and an evil eye a grasping and grudging one (Deut. 15:9; Prov. 23:6; 28:22). Even as men today speak of spiritual insight, so Jesus was insisting that a man could lose his sense of true values in life and become possessed by his possessions. (*The Zondervan Pictorial Encyclopedia of the Bible*, Merrill C. Tenney, editor, Zondervan, Vol. 5, p. 355)

4. Read Matthew 6:24. Which master would you rather serve, God or Money? Why?

5. Read Matthew 6:25-34. How many times are we told not to worry about food and clothes?

6. Do you have any anxieties? What are some of them?

7. What does verse 27 say about the benefits of worry?

8. What does the passage imply that we should be working for?

9. Restate the promise of verse 34 in your own words.

10. How do verses 33-34 sum up the previous verses?

11. What are some of your priorities? What are you accomplishing with your time? Are these things in line with what God has spelled out for us in Matthew 6:19-34? What will you do to rearrange your priorities, if that needs to be done?

# •TOOL CHEST•
*(A Suggested Optional Resource)*

## BIBLE ENCYCLOPEDIAS

Bible encyclopedias are multivolume sets of articles about people, places, and subjects arranged in alphabetical order (like a Bible dictionary). These articles go into much greater detail than those found in a Bible dictionary, however. They contain historical background information and sometimes even function as commentaries on the biblical books. Much helpful information is available in this type of Bible study tool. It is a great source to turn to and can save a lot of time and effort.

These sets, however, can be expensive—$100 or more—because they contain several volumes. *The Zondervan Pictorial Encyclopedia of the Bible,* edited by Merrill C. Tenney (Zondervan, 1975, 1976) is a five-volume set. Because of the great cost, it is unlikely that an individual would invest in one of these sets early on in the acquisition of a library. However, a church could add a set to the church library, or a group of people could invest in a set together. They may also be available at a public library or a college or university library.

A Bible encyclopedia is very easy to use. Simply look up the name, place, or subject you are interested in, and *read!*

# 7
# *Single Women*

## •FOOD FOR THOUGHT•

Mary Magdalene must be one of the most loved women of the Bible, yet she is probably one of the most misunderstood. Perhaps too many Bible women share her name for us to keep from distorting what we know about her. Mary is identified with her birthplace, Magdala, which was a popular, thriving town on the coast, three miles from Capernaum. There were a productive dye works and a textile industry there that no doubt contributed to the wealthy commerce that flowed from the city. Whether Mary was connected in any way with this busy industry is not certain, since we have no record of her marital status or her home background. We do know she was free to follow Jesus, indicating that she had no home ties and that she was perhaps single when she met the Lord.

Contrary to popular belief, Mary is not the same woman as the sinner woman we read about in Luke 7. There is no evidence that she was a prostitute. There are many reasons why such a tradition has grown up around Mary, but once the subject is investigated it is plain to see that she was a prominent, wealthy woman who was healed by Christ of terrible infirmities and who is named among the women of good reputation and means who ministered to Christ from their substance (Luke 8:1-3). Maybe the fact that the Scriptures introduce us to Mary following the story of the sinner woman in Simon the Pharisee's house has led some to the conclusion that this is the same lady, and perhaps the establishing of Magdalene houses by the Roman Catholic church to help girls of ill repute has helped maintain the confusion. I do not believe, however, that there is any scriptural evidence for such a view. There is no question that she was desperately tormented by demons. The Scriptures plainly spell that out (Luke 8:2). But that doesn't mean she was dissolute.

Trouble comes to all of us, even those with wealth and prominence, and Christ liberated Mary from her terrible trouble to be His particular blessing (Luke 8:1-3). She is shown in Scripture to be a woman of sacrifice, fortitude, and courage. She is mentioned fourteen times in the Gospel record and always in connection with other women. She invariably heads the list except at the cross, where it is obviously fitting that Mary the Lord's mother and other relatives should be mentioned first. She teaches us many things, not least the blessedness of being single and the advantage that the single lifestyle gives us to minister for Christ.

At this point some of you who are single may be saying, "That's all very well for you to say—you're married." Don't you just hate listening to talks about parenting given by people who don't have any kids, or homilies on singleness by people who are married? (Jesus, we need to remind ourselves, was not married and so knows all about it.) But in 1 Corinthians 7:29 we read that those of us who are married ought to live like those who are not! Those of us with partners are to cultivate a certain "single-mindedness" in our service for the Lord.

It is easy to see how the single person can give full attention to the Lord's service, but so should we who enjoy a marriage relationship. The situation, after all, is the same for all of us—the present crisis demands it, for the time is short. Paul was drawing attention to some dark clouds on the horizon. There were storms of persecution coming which could potentially engulf the church, and there was much to be done. People were lost but might be saved if they could hear the Gospel.

Today we are in the same situation. The time is still short. Half the world will never hear the Gospel; nine out of ten people are lost. Three-fourths of the world's population have yet to hear the Good News, and opposition to the faith grows.

First Corinthians 7 tells us that singleness is a precious gift. That is no doubt a new thought to many of us. Singleness, says Paul, is to be looked upon as a privilege rather than a punishment! "Each man has his own gift from God," explains the apostle, "one man has this gift, another has that" (1 Cor. 7:7, NIV). Gifts are to be accepted. It is extremely poor taste to refuse a gift—or worse still, to joke about it behind the giver's back. God calls us to accept the gift He gives us concerning our marital status: "each one should retain the place in life that the Lord assigned to him and to which God has called him" (1 Cor. 7:17, NIV). If singleness is indeed a gift and a calling, then we need to consider its usefulness. Singleness is a great position to be in because you don't have to stop what you're doing to get dinner, run kids to the soccer game, or go to the school sales. You can serve the Lord with unencumbered freedom. (I do not speak here of single parents but rather of singles who have never married.)

Being single can also mean less financial responsibility and as a result, a greater ability to give, which can be a great encouragement to God's servants who need support. Mary was apparently a lady of means. The Gospel cause calls for practical material gifts, and Mary had the ability to render that sort of service.

I don't know why it is, but there seems to be a tradition in Christian circles that giving God secondhand things is okay. When Stuart and I worked in a youth ministry we needed a piano. I put an advertisement in the paper and to my delight received a reply from a wealthy lady. "Jill, I've bought a new piano," she told me. "It's beautiful. I saw your ad in the paper so I'm calling to ask you if you would like our old one?" "No, thank you," I quickly replied, "I'd like your new one!" I didn't get either—which probably served me right for being so rude—but you know, I just got tired of God getting the old piano!

Why do we always give God the old piano? Of one thing I am sure, Mary Magdalene never did that! When the Bible says that the women who accompanied Jesus ministered to Him out of their substance, you can be sure they would be careful to give Him "the new piano"!

When Paul talks about singleness in 1 Corinthians 7:29-31, he says that because of the present crisis and our future prospects we should hold our possessions lightly and implies that we should give our gifts generously. It remains, he says, that "those who have wives should live as if they had none; those who mourn, as if they did not; those who are happy, as if they were not; those who buy something, as if it were not theirs to keep; those who use the things of the world, as if not engrossed in them. For this world in its present form is passing away" (1 Cor. 7:29-31, NIV). Likewise, Mary used her material resources, spending them for eternity.

Her single state also enabled her to attend upon the Lord without distraction, putting Jesus and His needs first and foremost in her life (1 Cor. 7:34). So often I hear people speak of what Jesus means to them, and of course that is perfectly valid. But Mary reminds us there is another way of looking at things. Have we ever asked ourselves, "What do I mean to Jesus?" That question is perfectly valid too! Mary's support of the Christ she loved was more than meaningful to Him. There is no doubt in my mind that her undivided devotion, single-hearted commitment, and practical help encouraged Him as He ministered. She served her Lord well in life.

It is not at all surprising that Mary also served Him well in death! On Easter Sunday morning we find Mary at the garden tomb, her hands full of costly ointments and spices, seeking to minister for the last time to Him whom she loved. She had come to make sure His body was prepared suitably for burial. She must have been very confused when she and the other women searched for Jesus' body and could not find it. Distraught, she stayed still in the garden, caring not if the authorities found and punished her for attending to the criminal's corpse.

Then He who valued her love so dearly bequeathed to Mary one of heaven's richest honors. She was to be the first to witness Him after His resurrection and the first to be commissioned to run and tell what she had seen and heard (John 20:11-17). Mary Magdalene was the first woman missionary and as such gives us a model of undivided commitment to Christ's cause. Singleness, God's great gift and calling to some, can be offered back to Jesus as a sweet gift of love. Be sure that He will be delighted to accept that costly present and you can know that you will bring unbounded joy to His heart!

# •TALKING IT OVER•

*Suggested Times*

---

1. READ AND SHARE.         *15 minutes*

   ☐ Read 1 Corinthians 7:8, 17-40. Discuss freely, keeping to the subject of single women, not marriage and divorce. Count the blessings of the single woman and share any testimonies from the group as illustrations.

   ☐ Read John 20:1-2, 10-18. What do these verses teach you about Mary? What do they teach you about you?

---

2. ACROSTIC.         *10 minutes*

Complete this acrostic of singleness as a group (or have each person take a letter).

| POSITIVES | NEGATIVES |
|---|---|
| Self-fulfillment | Survival |
| I | I |
| N | N |
| G | G |
| L | L |
| E | E |
| N | N |
| E | E |
| S | S |
| S | S |

---

3. PRAY.         *5 minutes*

# •PRAYING IT THROUGH•

*Suggested Times*

1. Using the acrostic from Talking It Over, praise God for the positives and pray to Him about the negatives.

    *5 minutes*

2. Pray for singles.
    ☐ Pray for single women you know who are struggling with their singleness (first names only).
    ☐ Pray for single missionaries.

    *5 minutes*

3. Pray for teenagers and college-age young people that they will have good biblical attitudes toward singleness. Use 1 Corinthians 7 to pray for them. For example, from verse 8: "Lord, help Ann to know it's a good thing to stay single—a privilege, not a punishment!"

    *5 minutes*

4. Read 1 Corinthians 7:29-31 aloud. Put yourself in these verses and pray for yourself.

    *5 minutes*

# •DIGGING DEEPER•

This lesson is a character study of a woman from the Old Testament—Rahab. The basic outline used in this lesson can be used to study any character in the Bible. The method is taken from a book called *12 Dynamic Bible Study Methods* by Richard Warren (Victor Books). Ten steps are included in the study. For this lesson the first two steps are already done for you.

Step one: Select the Bible person you want to study.
For this lesson, the person is Rahab.

Step two: Make a list of all the references about that person. Using a concordance, or, if you have a study Bible, an index, find all the Bible references you can about that person and things related to his life. For Rahab, the references are:

    Joshua 2:1-24       Hebrews 11:31
    Joshua 6:15-25     James 2:25

Step three: Write down first impressions (first reading). Read through the references you've listed and make some notes. Write out the first impression you have of this person. Then write down some basic observations and important information you discover about this person. Finally, list any problems, questions, or difficulties you wonder about as you read these references.

Step four: Make a chronological outline (second reading). Read all the references again and make a chronological outline of the person's life or of the events recorded in Scripture concerning the person.

Step five:  Get some insights into the person (third reading).
Go back over the references again and look for possible answers to these questions. Why do you think God
allowed this person to be mentioned in the Bible?

What were Rahab's motives?

What are the great accomplishments for which Rahab
is remembered?

What were the outstanding traits in Rahab's character?

What were Rahab's faults and weaknesses?

Did her life show any development of character as time passed? Was there growth and progression?

Was Rahab eager to do God's will, willingly and without question? What about the lie she told? Was it right or wrong? Discuss.

Step six:  Identify some character qualities (fourth reading). Read the references again, and list good and bad qualities that show up in the person's life. Give a verse reference that shows each characteristic.

Step seven:  Show how other Bible truths are illustrated in her life.
Examine the person's life to see how it illustrates other
truths taught in the Bible. For example, does her life
show the principle of "you will reap what you sow"?
Look for illustrations of some of the proverbs in this
person's life, and principles taught in the psalms. For
example, you might ask, "Does her life illustrate the
promise, "Delight yourself in the Lord and He will
give you the desires of your heart"? (Ps. 37:4, NIV)

Step eight:  Summarize the main lesson (or lessons).
In a few sentences write out what you think is the
main lesson that is taught or illustrated by this person's
life. Is there any one word that describes this person's
life? What was her outstanding characteristic?

Step nine:    Write out a personal application. Ask yourself these questions.

Did I see anything of myself in this person's life?
Did she show some of my weaknesses?
Did she reveal to me some of my strengths?
What impressed me most about this person's life?
Where do I fall short in this area?
What do I intend to do about it?

Step ten:    Make your study transferable.
Condense what you have learned into a simple outline that will help you remember it and enable you to share your conclusions with others. Make it "pass-on-able." Ask yourself, "What can this person's life mean to others? What can I share that I have learned that would help someone else?"

# •TOOL CHEST•
*(A Suggested Optional Resource)*

*12 DYNAMIC BIBLE STUDY METHODS*
The tool used in this lesson is *12 Dynamic Bible Study Methods* by Richard Warren (Victor Books, 1981). The book contains twelve different methods of approaching a Bible study. The method used in this study is found in Chapter 5, "A Biographical Method of Bible Study." The lesson here explains how to do the study—the book goes into a little more detail. The book is a paperback and is very reasonably priced, and it can be used by people at any level of Bible study experience.

Our lesson dealt with character studies; Warren in his book lists a number of books which are made up of Bible character studies. Some that deal exclusively with women are

*All the Women of the Bible,* Herbert Lockyer (Zondervan)
*All the Women of the Bible,* Edith Deen (Harper & Row)
*Her Name Is Woman,* books 1 & 2, Gien Karssen (NavPress)

# 8

# *Scheming Women*

## •FOOD FOR THOUGHT•

Not all the women in the life of the Lord Jesus were captivated by Him. Some that He met never responded to Him at all. Others were actively hostile. When Jesus came into Jairus' house the professional mourners laughed Him to scorn when He told them that Jairus' little daughter was not dead but rather sleeping. There were not only scornful women in Christ's life. I'm sure there were skeptical women too. There were even scheming women! It is to some of these manipulative women who stood in the shadows of the Saviour's life on earth that we now turn our attention.

The "royals" of Jesus' day were singularly unimpressed with religious reality. To understand why there were so many "rotten royals" cluttering up the landscape, we need to take a look at history.

Herod the Great was governor of Galilee when Christ was in His infancy. Records imply that Mariamne, one of Herod's wives, was the power behind the throne. The wives of all the ruling Herods played a huge role in the affairs of state one way or another, mainly because the women in question wanted very much to stay alive, and the only way to ensure that they did was to have an evil finger in the political intrigue that hung over their husbands' affairs. Mariamne was as intent as her husband on making sure power was kept firmly in the Herodian family hands, even though she knew very well that Herod did not have one single drop of Jewish blood in him.

Herod is said to have "loved" Mariamne, and she was probably the only human being he ever came close to loving, but he surely had a strange way of showing his affection! He became increasingly suspicious of any close relative who might conceivably have an eye on his crown, even having his two sons by Mariamne, Alexander and Aristobulus, put away for safety's sake.

As you can imagine, there were many plots against his life, but somehow he survived. Perhaps this was because he was not only the King of the Jews but the king of conspiracy and court intrigues too. He later became known as the Jewish Nero! Even cruel Caesar, after hearing about the execution of Herod's sons, remarked, "I would rather be Herod's hog than his son!" Despite the fact that her husband had murdered her whole family, Mariamne stuck by her husband, bound to him by her one burning ambition to hold onto the throne.

Now can you understand the impact the wise men had on the royal family the fateful day they arrived at the palace and were ushered into the King and Queen's presence? Consider the consternation when the wise men asked, "Where is He who has been born King of the Jews? For we have seen His star in the East and have come to worship Him." No wonder there was a massacre of innocent babies. Of course, we have to realize that the prince of evil sided with Herod the King. We read that he, Satan, was a murderer from the beginning (John 8:44). Seeing that the world system—that is, fallen humanity organized into tribes and nations—is under his jurisdiction, the life of God's Son, who had come to save the world, would obviously be a prime target. The King of God's kingdom lay helplessly in Mary's arms as Joseph hurriedly led them out of Herod's murderous path.

So Jesus never met the first scheming woman in His life, Mariamne. His God saved Him from destruction, for His time had not yet come. By the time Christ began His public ministry, the royals, true to form, were still totally unimpressed with religious reality. True, John the Baptist's preaching had caught the attention of Herod Antipas, son of Herod the Great. He loved to hear him preach and kept him handy, in prison, so he could have a private sermon whenever he felt like it (Mark 6:20).

John was in prison for daring to point out that Herodias, who had been seduced by Herod while on a trip to Rome, was his brother

Philip's wife, and the King had had no right to marry her. Herodias, of course, didn't appreciate his observations, and having raised a daughter as cruel and immoral as she, worked out a scheme to have John's head (Mark 6:21-28)! John the Baptist was an extremely popular and powerful leader. In Herodias' eyes, he needed to be removed. Knowing how the people hated the Herodian family, she and her husband could not afford to allow any man to become too popular with the people. Herodias dominated her husband and was bound and determined to do everything in her power to eliminate *any* who dared threaten their position.

Ask yourself now, if John was a threat to Herodias, how much more was Jesus? Do you think she was unaware of His popularity, of His miracles, of His claims to be a king? She would have her ear to the ground, and Jesus must have known His danger. The Herodian family had marked His life deeply already, forcing His family into exile in His childhood and murdering His beloved friend and cousin, John.

Herodias must have been happy at last when Jesus stood in front of Herod Antipas, as recorded in Luke 23. Herod, wanting Jesus to play magician, was disappointed and could not even get Jesus to say one word (Luke 23:9). If Herodias happened to be with Herod at that moment, I'm sure she would have enjoyed the soldiers' mocking of "the king" as they placed the broken reed in His hand, a symbol of broken power (Matt. 27:28-30).

Herodias had had her chance. She killed John and perhaps added to our Lord's torment on the way to His cross. Jesus had nothing else to say to her—a terrible thought!

Even after our Lord's death and resurrection, the women of the Herodian house haunted His life. His disciple James was killed by Herod's sword (Acts 12:2). We don't know the circumstances. Perhaps the Queen threw another party, and a daughter danced again. What we do know is that these scheming women kept their earthly thrones but lost their eternal souls. Today, Satan is still about his business—offering men and women the whole world if they will bow down and worship him.

We can find a way around the Lord's rules, or we can respond to His royal reign and recognize His rightful place on the throne of our lives. The choice is ours.

# •TALKING IT OVER•

| | |
|---|---|
| 1. READ AND SHARE. | *25 minutes* |

☐ In pairs, read Ephesians 6:10-13; 1 John 2:15-17; Matthew 6:24-34. As a group, discuss what these verses teach us about the world system organized by Satan and the one organized by God. What does the Bible tell us to do about this?

☐ Read Matthew 20:20-28. Using clues found in this story, discuss these questions: How do women scheme? Why do women scheme? When do women scheme?

☐ Read Philippians 2:1-11. Have volunteers put each of the verses in their own words. What are the differences between God's schemes and people's schemes?

| | |
|---|---|
| 2. PRAY. | *5 minutes* |

# •PRAYING IT THROUGH•

*Suggested Times*

1. Read Ephesians 6:10-12. Spend time praying about the things the evil powers are doing in the world. Claim God's victory in Jesus' name.

    *6 minutes*

2. Read Matthew 20:20. Pray about your own scheming nature.

    *6 minutes*

3. Read Ephesians 6:13-18. Pray about using the weapons of your warfare. Pray also for these warriors.
    ☐ Pastors
    ☐ Church leaders
    ☐ Missionaries

    *6 minutes*

4. Meditate silently.

    *2 minutes*

# •DIGGING DEEPER•

1. For background on the life of Jezebel, a scheming woman in the Old Testament, read these highlights and if you have time, the accompanying Scripture passages.
   - ☐ Wicked King Ahab marries Jezebel, a foreign woman, and begins to worship idols (1 Kings 16:29-34).
   - ☐ The Prophet Elijah tells Ahab that there will be no rain for several years (1 Kings 17:1).
   - ☐ God promises to send rain; meanwhile Jezebel kills many of the Lord's prophets (1 Kings 18:1-15).
   - ☐ God sends fire from heaven, which shows that He alone is Lord and Baal is not; Elijah kills the prophets of Baal (1 Kings 18:16-46).
   - ☐ Jezebel pledges to kill Elijah because he killed the prophets of Baal; Elijah flees into exile (1 Kings 19:1-18).
2. Read 1 Kings 21. Who are the people who play a part in this incident?

3. Write brief descriptions of each of the following persons' characters.
   Ahab:

   Naboth:

   Jezebel:

   Elijah:

4. Why do you think Naboth did not want to give up his vineyard?

5. The following excerpt is from *Eerdmans' Handbook to the Bible*, by David and Patricia Alexander, p. 268:
Seizure or compulsory purchase of land was illegal in Israel. A man's heritage had to be handed on to the next generation. But other people's rights do not bother Jezebel. While her husband sulks like a spoilt child, she quietly arranges for Naboth's liquidation. She has only to contrive a blasphemy charge—backed of course by the statutory number of witnesses—and the "criminal's" lands are forfeit.

When Naboth wouldn't sell his vineyard to Ahab, what did Jezebel do to acquire the vineyard? (1 Kings 21:1-16)

6. What do you think Jezebel *should* have done when Naboth refused to sell his vineyard?

7. What was God's response to Jezebel's scheming? (1 Kings 21:17-24)

8. When circumstances weren't going her way, Jezebel stopped at nothing in order to make them go her way. According to the following verses, what should *our* attitude be when things don't go the way we would like them to?
Proverbs 3:5-6

Matthew 6:33

Romans 8:28

Romans 12:1-2

9. King Saul schemed to kill David, God's choice for Saul's successor. How did David respond as King Saul was trying to kill him? (1 Samuel 26:1-11)

10. In what way do people try to manipulate other people or things so that circumstances will go their way?

11. What circumstances seem to be wrong in your life? How are you reacting? How *should* you be reacting?

# •TOOL CHEST•
*(A Suggested Optional Resource)*

### BIBLE HANDBOOK

A Bible handbook is similar to a Bible dictionary; the main difference is that a Bible dictionary has short articles arranged alphabetically, while a Bible handbook provides a brief running commentary on each of the books of the Bible. Many handbooks, such as *Eerdmans' Handbook to the Bible,* also contain articles about the Bible: how to use the Bible; historical background about the times, the authors, and the culture; and main themes in the Bible. *Eerdmans' Handbook* also contains tables of miracles and parables in the Bible, a "who's who," and a list of subjects and events. It is lavishly illustrated with photographs, drawings, and charts and is easy to understand, so that it would be suitable for use as a family devotional tool.